THE BLACK SEQUIN DRESS

Jenny Kemp

Current Theatre Series
Currency Press. Sydney
in association with
Playbox Theatre Centre, Monash University Melbourne

CURRENT THEATRE SERIES

First published in 1996 by
Currency Press Pty Ltd,
PO Box 452 Paddington
NSW 2021, Australia
in association with
Playbox Theatre Centre

National Library of Australia
Cataloguing-in-Publication data

Kemp, Jenny 1949-.
The black sequin dress.

ISBN 0 86819 466 2.

1. Playbox Theatre (Melbourne, Vic.). I.
Title. (Series: Current theatre series).

A822.3

Set by Currency, Paddington.
Printed by Bridge Printery.

Contents

The Black Sequin Dress was first produced by the
Adelaide Festival and the Playbox Theatre Centre at the
Adelaide Festival, on 5th March 1996 with the
following cast:

WOMAN 1	Margaret Mills
WOMAN 2	Helen Herbertson
WOMAN 3	Natasha Herbert
WOMAN 4	Mary Sitarenos
MAN	Ian Scott
WAITER	Greg Stone
GIRL'S VOICE	Romanie Harper

Director, Jenny Kemp
Composer, Elizabeth Drake
Designer, Jacqueline Everitt
Lighting designer, Ben Cobham

For Richard

CAST

WOMAN IN BLACK SEQUIN DRESS 1
WOMAN IN BLACK SEQUIN DRESS 2
WOMAN IN BLACK SEQUIN DRESS 3
WOMAN IN BLACK SEQUIN DRESS 4
WAN IN A FORMAL SUIT
WAITER IN A FORMAL SUIT
VOICE OF A YOUNG GIRL

MAIN ACTIONS

Actual action
Fantasy action
Remembered action
Dream action
Mythic action

SETTING

Images to be used in the play are inspired by the paintings of Paul Delvaux.

The setting is a nightclub with a shiny floor. Into this space run two tunnels. The upstage tunnel has a railway track which runs straight across the nightclub floor. A train with several carriages runs through the nightclub for some sequences. The back wall of the nightclub consists of a large white wall which can become a wall of light, or can be projected onto for the country walk sequences. Stage right, about halfway upstage, is a rectangle of earth where the woman lies down to sleep. At the front sides of the nightclub, facing towards the audience, are two fairly wide doorways marked exit. We are able to see into these areas a little but most of the action in these areas takes place just near or in the doorway. Above the stage right door is a longish vertical window behind which someone may stand. Above the stage left door is a long horizontal window or box in which lies a figure looking either asleep or dead.

SEQUENCES OF EVENTS

SEQUENCE A: THE GESTALT

Undine's Story Part One: the brick wall
Nightmare 1
It's as if my body has been taken apart
Arriving at the Nightclub: Entrance 1 – the setting
AZB Memory – demonstration
Fantasy Conversation: the fall
Myth 1: Memory – crossing the River Styx
Arriving at the Nightclub: Entrance 2 – just the walk
Nightmare 2
Country Walk 1: collapses and sobs
Fantasy Conversation: start the day with you
Fantasy Dance 1: the maduri delight
Myth 2: Crossing the River Styx – Help me I'm
     drowning
Arriving at the Nightclub: Entrance 3 – relax
Fantasy Conversation: on train – Excuse me your name
     isn't Gary is it?
Dictionary Definition: to fall – your hand touches me
Fantasy Conversation: on train – Excuse me your name
     isn't Gary is it? (continued)
Memory: dogs
Memory: In the kitchen – the lino looks dull
Myth 3: Crossing the River Styx – the dogs

SEQUENCE B: GOING DOWN

Nightmare 3
Country Walk 2: steep descent
Arriving at the Nightclub: Entrance 4 – the men / dice
     play / chaos theory
Fantasy Dance 2: the Goths

SEQUENCE A: THE GESTALT

UNDINE'S STORY PART ONE

We see bricks (a projected image 1 min 45 sec). WOMAN 1, *wearing a simple day dress, is standing centre in front of the brick wall. She remains still. The text is spoken from off by* WOMAN 3.

WOMAN 3 [*voice over*]: Undine lives in the suburbs in a commission home. A brick one. All the houses in Undine's street are the same with just slight variations, so you want to go into other people's houses to spot the difference. Undine closes her eyes to the bricks and finds herself in a flat land. She gazes at the horizon but oddly it does not appear distant, she looks down and sees her two feet, they look as if they are standing on the horizon. Has she grown tall, or have they receded? She cannot look into the depth of the landscape, she stands on it. She stands on a flat plane, she may as well be standing inside a perspex cube. She puts out her hand to test the space in front of her. Nothing, just air of a medium temperature or even of no temperature at all. She waves her arm, it moves jerkily, it is a message from her brain, she knows telling her arm to move and wave, as if someone is standing at a distance outside her cube and needs to be acknowledged. Her arm goes down, her knees bend and she keels over, she faints off the edge of the earth, she falls out of the dead landscape. Her body crumples to the ground, her head falls back against the hard earth, earth as hard as stone, ping like a metal ball it bounces for a moment and falls still.

> [*There is a pause.* WOMAN 1 *remains standing and then collapses to the floor. The bricks fall (the cyc should fall slightly behind her.) There is stillness.* WOMAN 3, *in a black satin wide strap slip, is lying asleep on the earth.* WOMAN 4,

in the same day dress as WOMAN 1, *stands at the right exit door embracing a skeleton. We see its back and her front. We now also see the horizontal box above the left exit.*]

NIGHTMARE 1

After a short period WOMAN 3 *wakes with a gasp. She sits up trying to orientate.*

WOMAN 3: What's that! What was that scream?
[*She looks behind her.*]
I thought I heard a scream.
[*She is shaking.*]
I need a drink of water. I think I fell, or someone fell.
[*Pause.*]
I need some water.
[*She takes a glass from the floor beside her and drinks.*]

IT'S AS IF MY BODY HAS BEEN TAKEN APART

WOMAN 4 *speaks the text as the bricks slide from the stage.* WOMAN 1 *slowly gets up and leaves the stage by the left exit. The train (with facade up) slides slowly from the right tunnel across stage and into the opposite tunnel. In the first carriage we see the* MAN *and the* WAITER, *both with hats and jackets, sitting opposite each other at a small table having a drink. It is daytime and it is the buffet car.* WOMAN 2, *also in the day dress, begins to walk from the front end of the train past the* MEN *towards the second carriage. As she passes them she slips and nearly falls. She steadies herself on their table. The* WAITER *helps her. They exchange glances. She then looks at the* MAN, *who is facing the front of the train, and continues to her carriage. She sits at her table, drinks some water, then turns and looks out the window as the train leaves the stage.*

WOMAN 4: It's as if my body had been taken apart and put together again. One part separated from another, all floating, speeding off, as if bombed, shooting out into the darkness, the

2

universe, and put together again. Again as if all this may have happened many times before. Something better this time, put together, by the force of the return flight, after the bombing which had just occurred. A shock which something in me knows all about. But now I don't. What could it be? – a memory – which returned with an incredible force, fell, or was propelled from one area into another, somewhere where it had been tightly held. Perhaps there was a kind of explosion in this area which set it free, or maybe just things changed ...

[*The train disappears.*]

... then the shock was the new arrangement. Something completely different after all these years.

[WOMAN 3 *leaves by downstage left tunnel.*]

THE WOMAN IN THE BLACK SEQUIN DRESS ARRIVES AT THE NIGHTCLUB

ENTRANCE 1 – THE SETTING

We hear music and the WAITER *appears and stands by the wall in between the front and back left tunnels.* WOMAN 1, *now in a black sequin dress, enters from the upstage left tunnel, pauses at doorway, walks into the nightclub and down centre stage to the front as she speaks the following text. The* MAN *enters from the upstage left tunnel and stands a little way along the track with his back to the audience as if waiting for the train.*

WOMAN 1: I can see a beautiful nightclub. Black shiny surfaces, all polished and clean, sparkling glasses full of champagne, gin and tonic, cocktails, liqueurs etc. Women melting into their partners bodies, the men wrapped around them like blankets. The band, in a row laid back, handsome. Snacks, cards, cigarettes, money, lipstick, watches, jewellery, high stools, dancing, wild dancing, bare bodies under not much. They abandon themselves here. Get out of their day shoes and set off at a gallop, drinks whizzing down the gullet, talk gurgling up, hands wandering all over the place, anywhere will do, who cares. They have learned how not to care, how here to let go the reins.

[WOMAN 3 *appears in the entrance of the downstage right tunnel with glass of water and watches.*]

They want to show off, they want to fall in love with the moment and it to fall in love with them. Greedy are they? No, not greedy. Hungry.

[*The* MAN *enters.*]

I love, I love, I love love they think. Love me, me, me, me, all of me. Fill me up, fill me up. I've had a bath, I've put on my deodorant, my clothes are impeccable. Now now now do the next bit, come over they seem to be screaming.

Come over here and really fill me up with something significant something – of value.

A right word a soft word at just the right moment straight down the ear hole, ping bullseye, right to the hungry spot, ping and then ah, ah, that was it. Got it thank you, now anything I can do for you back? No, yes, not a sure thing at all, perhaps not.

[*The* WOMAN *has arrived centre front. She stops.*]

Or someone could walk up their timing perfect, and stand fitting the shape of me. Perfection, it would register. I would breath out, relax and they would sit and put a hand out somewhere on the table, it would contact my hand and ping down the arm would go, the message and it would run up the shoulder into the head, down whiz straight to the heart and zoom, zing the genitals aflame. And my dress would fill up with light. I would wake up and dance I would jump off the end of the pier, free fall. And he would fly over the end after me splash, gurgle gurgle gurgle. And down we go.

[*She pauses, looks back over her right shoulder. At this moment she is suddenly thrown off balance. Her left foot slips and her body crumples to the floor. As she falls,* WOMAN 2 *enters from the upstage right tunnel. She is wearing a black sequin dress and holding an owl. She walks downstage by the tunnels.* WOMAN 3 *enters from upstage right tunnel and stands on the earth.*]

4

WOMAN 4 *speaks the the following text as looking out the window.
The following actions occur simultaneously. The* WAITER *moves
into action, addressing* WOMAN 1, *"Madam, are you all right?!"
She stirs then looks up. He helps her to a chair by the left wall,
offers her a drink. She says, "Yes." He takes one off the wall for
her. She drinks and hands the glass back to the* WAITER. *He leaves.
The* MAN *turns and walks to the centre front spot. From there he
goes and sits on the left chair. When* WOMAN 1 *returns to the chair
he gets up and stands by the downstage left wall, then leaves by the
left exit. He repeats this pattern, then a little later appears on his
upstage left spot. The train enters from the left tunnel (with facade
off, two seats in the first carriage and an enormous ball in the
second). It stops centre stage.* WOMAN 2 *immediately walks to
centre front, pauses, looks at the spot where* WOMAN 1 *fell, then
walks straight upstage. She turns and walks back to the front, then
walks slowly back to the train. The ball rolls out of the train and*
WOMAN 3 *hurries to pick it up. She bounces it, then puts it back on
the train and gets on herself.* WOMAN 1 *gets up, walks to the centre
spot, walks upstage back to the front and then to her chair. Then*
WOMAN 2 *gets on the train as it moves off through the right tunnel.
The others move aside for her to sit.*

WOMAN 4: Brownian movement is the zigzag movement of tiny
particles like dust motes as they are buffeted by collisions with
molecules of a gas or a liquid. It is out there in nature and
apparently available to observation. You can watch those little
motes zigzagging around before your eyes.

   [*The train stops.*]
Can you really?
   [*The ball rolls out.*]
What you see during any observation are two positions of your
mote – a "before" and an "after." Say it goes from point A to
point B. If you make more frequent observations of your mote,
you will discover that in going from point A to point B,

[*Ball back on.*]

... it goes from point A to point Z.

[MAN *gets on train.*]

... and then to point Y and *then* to point B. What is curious and a little frightening ...

[*Train moves.* WOMAN 2 *gets on.*]

... is that every time you make your observation more precise, you discover new zigzags – and the increasing complexity of the movement seems to have no limit.

FANTASY CONVERSATION WITH THE WOMAN IN THE BLACK SEQUIN DRESS

THE FALL

WOMAN 1 *is standing, considering leaving, when the* WAITER *enters from the left tunnel to fill glasses on the right wall. He glances back at* WOMAN 1. *They begin to talk.* WOMAN 2 *walks through the upstage tunnel with a tea cup and saucer.*

WOMAN 1: How awful, to have fallen.

WAITER: Yes.

WOMAN 1: Thank you for so quickly coming to the rescue. I was thrown, I'm not used to falling like that. It's a humiliating thing to fall like a child in such an adult setting.

[*Pause. The* MAN *appears and stands on his upstage spot, back to the audience.*]

I wonder whether I will dare to dance.

WAITER: There was no one here to see.

[*Pause.*]

WOMAN 1: But you.

WAITER: Ah yes, but me.

WOMAN 1: What did you see?

WAITER: I saw a woman walking across the floor. She tripped and fell in a flying movement, no I think she slipped and fell backwards ... [*Demonstrates*] ... she threw out her arms, as her body landed it must have been with a thud. Her spine unravelled backwards and then she went still.

[*The* MAN *exits through the upstage right tunnel.*]

WOMAN 1: For long? Was I still on the floor for long?

WAITER: No, no just a split second or a couple of seconds.

    [*Pause.*]

    Perhaps I imagined that you had died.

    [*Pause.*]

    I'm sure you'll find it safe to dance.

WOMAN 1: Yes. Could you bring me another drink, please.

WAITER: Certainly madam.

    [*He leaves.*]

MYTH 1: MEMORY – CROSSING THE RIVER STYX

We hear the words, "I mustn't look, I mustn't look", then WOMAN 4
*enters from the backstage left tunnel, carrying a box. She continues
to speak as she walks to backstage centre where she stops and turns
to look at the place where* WOMAN 1 *fell. She watches the floor as
the following scene takes place. We hear the texts simultaneously,*
WOMAN 3 *speaks as she embraces the* MAN *(a realistic dummy) in
the right exit door. We see the back of his body and her front. She is
listening to the girl's voice as she speaks. Every now and then she
stops to hear more clearly. We see the body lying above the left exit
door where* WOMAN 2 *stands with a cup and saucer. She places the
cup and saucer on the floor then lies down trying to remember the
position of the mother's body. She then gets up, looks at the saucer
and leaves.*

GIRL'S VOICE [*voice over*]: Mum, mum, mum. Down down down,
    she's fallen through the lino floor. I'll have to go straight down
    after her, can't live without her, she must be hiding under the
    lino. How can I get down there? Lie down, lie down, lie down
    stupid. I can't, I can't move, my feet are glued to the lino. Mum
    Mum Mum my voice won't come out. I'm dying. I'm dying
    alive, standing alive, I'm dead, dead. I'm dead.

WOMAN 3: Looking out the back window to see the lovely day, the
    sun on the boring grass, nothing there, nothing it's all just
    slowly and sucessfully growing while you are ... It comes the
    day like a blind force and I have to close my eyes. It all looks so

7

sure of itself, yet nowhere can I see you. Just grass and trees and plants eating up the earth. The desert has eaten me.

[WOMAN 4 *walks off.*]

THE WOMAN IN THE BLACK SEQUIN DRESS ARRIVES AT THE NIGHT CLUB

ENTRANCE 2 – JUST THE WALK

We hear music. WOMAN 2, *in a back seuqin dress, enters. She walks quite fast down the same path as* WOMAN 1. *She also stops centre front, turns, slips and falls. She remains on the floor. The train appears from right tunnel (facade off).* WOMAN 3 *is aboard. She is asleep. She wakes as the train goes across the stage.*

NIGHTMARE 2

WOMAN 3: What's that! What was that scream? I thought I heard a scream.

[*She is shaking.*]

I need a drink of water. I think I fell, or someone fell.

[*Pause.*]

I need some water.

[*The train disappears.*]

COUNTRY WALK 1: COLLAPSES AND SOBS

A film projection establishes of a tree blowing in the wind (2 min 15 secs). WOMAN 3 *speaks the text (from a microphone offstage) as* WOMAN 4 *enters from the upstage left tunnel. She walks slowly and with extreme tiredness between the tracks towards stage right. She is carrying a box.* WOMAN 2 *gets up, goes and picks up the tea cup and saucer and leaves.* WOMAN 1 *walks across the floor and stands by the earth. When* WOMAN 4 *is only a few metres from the right tunnel she stops in her tracks. The* WAITER *enters.*

WOMAN 3 [*voice over*]: In the landscape the ball of Undine's foot lands softly inside her sock, as her boot flattens across the earth. Her eyes travel from the stalks of straw like grass up over the expanse of the earth into the dense foliage and disappear inside the darkness. She floats across the landscape and finds herself lying in a horizontal position in the dark, along a branch. She is suitably light as a feather and balances without danger of falling. She gazes up through the trees and sees high above the branches the leaves battered by the wind. She travels without the distraction of footsteps below. Her feet are very still inside her boots, her hair moves forward around her face, she looks out and gazes into the distance. Her eyes shift focus and take in the depth of the landscape, she stirs deep inside, Woman 1 walks with tension to the earth and crumples down. She takes two definite and defiant steps forward, as if a sudden burst of courage has enabled her to advance. She sees that now the landscape in front of her has changed shape. Her face changes as she walks, her body becomes less upright her lips tremble her eyes moisten, she collapses onto the grass and sobs.

[*The film disappears.*]

FANTASY CONVERSATION WITH THE WOMAN IN THE BLACK SEQUIN DRESS

START THE DAY WITH YOU

The WAITER *enters with a tray, an exotic drink on it. He addresses* WOMAN 1. WOMAN 4 *remains looking straight ahead.*

WAITER: Start the day with you, and not the fears of yesterday.
WOMAN 4: How true.
WAITER: Simply get up and walk forward one foot after another.
WOMAN 4: How lovely you make it sound.
WAITER: Invent a point somewhere on the horizon.
    [WOMAN 1 *faces the front.*]
WOMAN 4: Ah yes, the horizon. I feel as if I do just the opposite.

[WOMAN 4 *leaves. The* WAITER *holds out the tray.*]

WAITER: A new drink?

WOMAN 1: Change drinks?

WAITER: Yes.

WOMAN 1: To what?

WAITER: Oh, a maduri delight?

WOMAN 1: Oh.

WAITER: But you agree.

WOMAN 1: Yes, I'll do it.

    [*She takes the drink. The* WAITER *holds out his hand.*]

WAITER: I'm Raymond.

WOMAN 1: [*takes his hand*] Angelica.

WAITER: A drink and then a dance.

    [*He backs off into the tunnel as we hear music and see the others dance on from the right exit.*]

The trail behind you will be there whether you watch it or not.

    [*He leaves.*]

FANTASY DANCE 1: THE MADURI DELIGHT

The dancers cross and disappear into the left exit. They reappear and dance along the downstage tunnel. There is a transition here into the Crossing the River Styx scene. We see the odd dancer with a loaf or the box, then the nightclub disappears and the tunnels appear.

MYTH 2: CROSSING THE RIVER STYX – HELP ME I'M DROWNING

We hear a horrifying old male voice screaming.

MALE VOICE: Help me!
  Please help me!
  Please help me into the boat
  Please save me,
  I'm drowning!

[WOMEN 2, 3 & 4 *are hurrying along the tunnels.* WOMAN 2 *and* WOMAN 3 *carry a loaf of bread in each hand and a coin in their mouths. They are on a treacherous journey.* WOMAN 4 *carries a box. We hear the sound of a river. The* WOMEN *hurry on, not allowing themselves to be affected by the call for help. After several crossings,* WOMAN 1 *follows one of the women off. The* MAN *enters towards the end of this sequence and stands in his former position upstage left, his back to the audience.* WOMAN 3 *stops with her loaf just in front of the earth. Her body is full of tension. The* WAITER *helps her onto the earth, takes the loaf and leaves.*]

THE WOMAN IN THE BLACK SEQUIN DRESS ARRIVES AT THE NIGHTCLUB

ENTRANCE 3 – RELAX

The train (facade off) enters slowly from the left tunnel and stops centre stage. WOMAN 1 *and* WOMAN 4 *are sitting on the train opposite each other, both wearing black sequin dresses.* WOMAN 4 *descends from the train, glances at the* MAN *and then repeats the entrance walk and fall.* WOMAN 1 *speaks the following text as she watches her from the train.* WOMAN 2 *watches from the left chair.*

WOMAN 1: Allow yourself to relax, relax and let yourself experience your own internal rhythm. Let your muscles go, let go your diaphragm. Soften your upper chest so your diaphragm can release, so you can be breathed.
   [*The train moves off slowly to the right tunnel. The* MAN *gets on as it moves.*]
Trust the stillness inside your body, you won't die.
   [WOMAN 3 *relaxes. The* WAITER *takes the bread and leaves.*]
Soften in the middle of your chest allow your heart space to expand, to soften. Relax on either side of the spine. Relax. Soften your eyelids, allow your head to relax. Allow your whole body to be breathed. Let your eyes look, let your ears hear and proceed like that.
   [*The train has gone.* WOMAN 4 *stops, turns and falls.*]

11

FANTASY CONVERSATION WITH THE WOMAN IN THE BLACK SEQUIN DRESS

ON TRAIN – EXCUSE ME YOUR NAME ISN'T GARY IS IT?

The train enters from the right tunnel (facade up). WOMAN 4 *remains on the floor as* WOMAN 1 *and the* MAN *speak the following text. The train moves across and into the opposite tunnel. The* WAITER *enters from the right exit and smokes.* WOMAN 2 *becomes uncomfortable, looks for the exit, finds it, then looks across at the* WAITER. *She holds his gaze for a moment and then leaves by the left exit.*

WOMAN 1: Excuse me your name isn't Gary is it?

MAN: No. I'm Raymond.

WOMAN 1: Ray for short?

MAN: Yes.

WOMAN 1: Ray is a wonderful name as a ray is such a positive thing.

MAN: How do you mean?

WOMAN 1: A ray of light, that sort of thing. But you do look very like a past acquaintance of mine called Gary.

> [WOMAN 3 *leaves by the upstage right tunnel.*]

MAN: Ah. Well I'm flattered. And your name?

WOMAN 1: Janice ... Madeleine ... But to tell you the truth I always wished my name had been Raelene. So aren't you lucky.

MAN: Lucky?

WOMAN 1: To have been a boy who was named Raymond.

MAN: I suppose so.

> [*Pause.*]

What would you name me if I was your baby?

WOMAN 1 [*she smiles, considers*]: You're such a big baby, I'd have to consider that.

MAN: True.

12

WOMAN 1: Let me see. Am I as the pretend mother from anywhere exotic?

MAN: My mother is English and my father is Russian.

WOMAN 1: Russian? I would love to be Russian for a change.

[*Pause.*]

Rudy.

MAN: Not Rudolf.

[*The train disappears.*]

WOMAN 1: Vladimir, but perhaps I won't remain your mother Vladimir.

MAN: No of course not Raelene.

DICTIONARY DEFINITION: TO FALL – YOUR HAND TOUCHES ME

There is silence. WOMAN 4 *lifts her head, orientates, looks from side to side and behind her. She finds herself alone, gets up, stands, thinks, then very slowly turns just her head and then upper body to the back. She is remembering and examining the fall. She then re-enacts the fall extremely slowly. As she does this we hear the dictionary definition (from offstage microphone), spoken by* WOMAN 3. *After* WOMAN 4 *lands on the floor, "Your hand touches me" is spoken simultaneously by the* WAITER *(from off) with the rest of the dictionary definition as she gets up, slowly makes her way to the stage left chair and sits down.*

WOMAN 1: Fall away: fall back: fall out: fall among: fall behind: fall down: fall flat: fall in: fall off: fall on one's feet: fall over: fall over backwards: fall over oneself: fall short: to free fall. To descend: to throw oneself down: to be dropped in birth: to collapse: to die away: to sink: to drop dead: to be overthrown: to come to ruin: to lose power:

[*Her head finally lands on the floor. The second text begins and the dictionary definition. Continues very intermittently.*]

... to be degraded: to become a victim: to yield to temptation: to begin to be: fall asleep, fall in love: to find place ...

WAITER: Your hand touches me, you touch me, touch me. you touch me you you you touch me me, your arm, your fingers, your heart behind them all, your head your eyes your mind all together touch me. Your fingertips stroke me, I change, I change as you stroke me with your touch. Your eyes closed, with your eyes open, you touch me. I shift I change. I shift under your heart under the touch of your fingertips your eyes. I slip off into you into me into thank god somewhere else. You are everywhere but not in the way you are, your touch, in me, on me, in me, on me.

FANTASY CONVERSATION WITH THE WOMAN IN THE BLACK SEQUIN DRESS

ON TRAIN – EXCUSE ME YOUR NAME ISN'T GARY IS IT? (CONTINUED)

The train enters from the left tunnel (facade up). It goes by quite quickly. The MAN *and* WOMAN 1 *are now sitting in the first carriage opposite each other at a table with a small lamp. The second carriage, also with table and lamp, is empty. They continue their previous conversation which is now midstream.* WOMAN 4, *who is exhausted, slightly dozes off.*

WOMAN 1: I can see that you don't let the past cause you much pain.
 A no regrets man I would say. A man of action.
MAN: I'm not entirely without empathy however.
WOMAN 1: Or would you even be here.
MAN: I will learn to suffer.
WOMAN 1: You are right ahead of me now.
MAN: But you haven't said yes.
WOMAN 1: No but I have relaxed. You've no idea how seldom I
 relax.
 [*The train disappears through the downstage right tunnel.*]

MEMORY: DOGS

Meanwhile WOMAN 4 *has dozed off on her chair and the* WAITER *has crawled in as a dog. He nuzzels her on the ankle. She screams in shock and panic, leaps up and runs downstage right, away from the 'dog'. He pursues her barking fiercely. She falls down and crawls, panic stricken, away. He catches up and barks over her frozen body. She makes an escape through the right tunnel. He pursues.*

MEMORY: IN THE KITCHEN – THE LINO LOOKS DULL

WOMAN 3 *stands embracing the* MAN *in the right exit.* WOMAN 2 *stands in the left exit. She has a cup of tea. She lies down, simulating the mother's position, then leaves. We see the body lying above the exit. These two texts are heard simultaneously.* WOMAN 3 *listens to the child's voice as she speaks. Sometimes she stops to listen more intently.* WOMAN 1 *enters, takes a glass of water from the wall, drinks and goes and lies down on the earth. She tosses and turns in her sleep. On the sill of the small window we see a model of the Earth and Moon phases.*

WOMAN 3: Looking out the back window to see the lovely day, the sun on the boring grass, nothing there, nothing it's all just slowly and sucessfully growing while you are ... It all looks so sure of itself, yet nowhere can I see you. The desert has eaten me. Dead flowers in the vases, the children away, the huge indoor plant seeming to get bigger by the second, the biggest thing in the house. I thought I will never be able to move.

CHILD'S VOICE [*voice over*]: The lino looks dull. She hasn't polished it for a long time. Is she breathing? I can't get the fruit cake out of my mind, the way it bounced on the floor when we dropped it. Why doesn't she wake up? Mum. Perhaps I'll get a glass of milk while I wait for her. I can't move. It's started

15

raining. She's got stockings on and it's so hot. Her handbag looks as if she put it there deliberately. I wonder what stockings feel like? I don't want to wear them. Did she fall? Or lie down because she was hot?

MYTH 3: CROSSING THE RIVER STYX – THE DOGS

We hear the sound of water and a horrifying old male voice screaming, "Help me I'm drowning" etc. as before, and many dogs barking fiercely. WOMAN 2 *appears with bread and coins, walking quickly at first through the tunnels. She is approaching the dogs. The barking gets louder and* WOMAN 2 *more terrified.* WOMAN 1 *gets off the earth and runs off. She runs through the downstage tunnel with the bread and then lies back on the earth.* WOMAN 2 *eventually slows down and throws the bread to the dogs. The barking gets more fierce as she runs back as fast as possible, slipping and falling several times as she runs. The barking dies down. Towards the end the* MAN *enters and stands on his upstage spot, back to audience, still calling for help.*

SEQUENCE B: GOING DOWN

NIGHTMARE 3

WOMAN 1 *screams and sits up suddenly. The* MAN *slowly turns just his head and looks at the centre front spot.*

WOMAN 1: What's that! [*To herself*] What was that scream?
   [*She looks behind her.*]
I thought I heard a scream.
   [*She is shaking.*]
I need a drink of water. I think I fell, or someone fell.
   [*Pause.*]
I need some water.

COUNTRY WALK 2: STEEP DESCENT

We see a projected film of a descent into dense bush (1min 45 sec). WOMAN 4 *speaks text from an offstage microphone. The* MAN *walks along the* WOMAN'*s path to the centre front. His head is down. He is examining her tracks. He stops at the front, examines the action of the fall, then steps to the side and looks at the path, then up to the projection. Meanwhile the* WAITER *has entered from the right exit, head down, thinking and ends up standing still and looking at the* MAN'*s profile.* WOMAN 1 *remains sitting on the earth and watches the* MAN.

WOMAN 4 [*voice over*]: Undine leans backwards to balance her body against the steep descent her hands part the dense undergrowth moving branches and bracken aside while her leg steps forward into the space created, her eyes glance quickly below and search for movement, for eyes, for holes, for leeches, for plants with unexpected prickles, then her leg follows landing sideways on the steep slope. Her other hand searches above her to make sure nothing will land in her face. Her whole body is in action, with the branches and the slope. She is poised on the edge at every moment, she is on her way down into the gully. She travels down towards the leech filled stream at the bottom. Her legs are stretched to their limit, her muscles flexed to balance the weight of her body down the steep incline. There is now a film of sweat on her skin and around her hair is damp from effort.

THE WOMAN IN THE BLACK SEQUIN DRESS ARRIVES AT THE NIGHTCLUB

NIGHTCLUB ENTRANCE 4 – THE MEN / DICE PLAY / CHAOS THEORY

We see the MEN *standing in stillness. We hear music.* WOMAN 2 *appears at window. The* MAN *eventually turns towards the* WAITER. *He has a dice shaker in his hand. The* WAITER *goes and gets a table. He puts it down centre stage. The* MAN *rolls some dice as the* WAITER *goes off for a couple of drinks. He returns and they begin to play a dice game. During this sequence the following actions occur simultaneously.* WOMAN 3, *in a black sequin dress, enters from the upstage left tunnel and down the centre path. She stops centre stage and watches the* MEN *with fascination. She remains still for the whole sequence.* WOMAN 1 *becomes interested in the* MEN'*s game and goes up and watches them. She plays with the* MAN *as he rolls dice, a hand aroud his neck, then waist etc. He mostly completely ignores this but does not seem to mind either. At one point she may make him smile for a moment. She also has a roll of the dice. The* MEN *are mostly interested in the dice. Just every now and then the text is spoken. An odd comment about the game may be improvised here. It is quite a long scene. The game expands as the dice throwing causes the dice to roll onto the floor.*

MAN: Of course, you do not have to choose between absolute disorder and absolute order.

[*Pause. They keep rolling throughout the scene.*]
In Mozart's "Dice Play" the disorder acts as a dash of seasoning to the order.
[*Pause.*]
There are patterns of randomness as well as simple randomness,
[*Pause.*]
... and chaos theory –
WAITER [*pause*]: – which is related to fractal geometry.
MAN [*continues*]: ... explores situations in which order is born from disorder ...
[*Pause. Looks at the unfavourable result of his dice throw.*]
... and disorder from order.
WAITER: The microcosm, the macrocosm.
MAN: The configuration above.
[*Gestures up.*]
And the configuration below.
[*Gestures below, then pauses and thinks.*]
So to speak.
[*Pause. Continues to roll dice.*]
Well.
[*Pause. WOMAN 2 takes the skeleton and leaves.*]
The pattern on a beetle's back.
[*Pause.*]
Or daisies in a cow paddock.
[*Pause. WOMAN 4 looks for the exit and leaves.*]
Then, the cow pat.
[*Gestures.*]
Pht! Gone.
[*There is stillness. The game is finished. The MAN stares at the dice. WOMAN 1 takes the dice and the shaker, the WAITER takes the empty glasses, the MAN snaps out of it, picks up the table, looks at WOMAN 1 and exits by the downstage left tunnel singing "Day and Night". WOMAN 1 goes off with him. The WAITER stands lost in thought, then he leaves by the right tunnel, humming the same tune as the MAN. WOMAN 1 then leaves.*]
MAN: Day and night, night and day, it hurts to be in love this way ...
[WOMAN 3 *finds herself alone, stuck halfway to her table.*]
WOMAN 3: What am I thinking stopping in the middle of the floor. I've stopped. I can't go on, I'm stuck. I feel as if someone is

behind me, creeping up, are they going to bash me over the head. I can't hear anything. This is not a good idea. I'll just slip back out.

[*She walks backwards, then stops herself.*]

Make yourself choose a table.

[*Pause.*]

Good that one, it is a long way, but yes that one, it is towards a corner. Just walk across the floor to it now. Go move walk one foot forward after another.

[*She begins walking again.*]

Keep moving, you of all people know how to walk. It's like walking on an ice rink. Ah yes I love it. I'm striding out, my dress feels right I'm relaxed. I'm all alone and complete. Step step step step, I'm almost dancing.

[*She glances back and falls.*]

FANTASY DANCE 2: THE GOTHS

WOMAN 3 *remains as a group of people walk/dance in beat from the downstage right tunnel across to the downstage left area. The* WAITER *hurries across, addresses her with his usual words and helps her to the chair. Meanwhile the group have all stopped and turned and are now 'marching' back to the right tunnel where they stop again, turn and take off in various directions slightly echoing the ABZ sequence. After several crossings they leave by the downstage left tunnel. The* WAITER *enters with a jug and goes past* WOMAN 3 *down stage left to refill glasses. During the following conversation the* WAITER *fills glasses along the walls, ending up opposite her by the right wall. A little way into the conversation* WOMEN 4, 2 *and* 1 *enter from the upstage left tunnel and stand at the back with tea cups, watching.*

FANTASY CONVERSATION WITH THE WOMAN IN THE BLACK SEQUIN DRESS

DEAD BODY

WOMEN 1, 2 *and* 4 *enter from upstage left. tunnel and stand holding tea cups and saucers. They stand together upstage watching and listening to the following scene.* WOMAN 4 *is upstage centre,* WOMAN 1 *is upstage left with* WOMAN 2 *slightly behind her.*

WOMAN 1: In the city last night I saw a dead body. It was out of the river, naked, a woman's body. Slightly blue. I thought it could have been me, yet here I was the one standing watching.

WAITER: A dead body. I've never seen a dead body.

WOMAN 1: I've been a dead body for some time.

WAITER: I look at you and see nothing dead at all. I see a woman sitting having a drink and chatting to me. I can imagine you running and jumping, walking briskly, dancing laughing eating.

WOMAN 1: Sleeping can you imagine me sleeping? Would I be allowed to sleep.

WAITER: Close your eyes.

[*She does.*]

Long lashes, you seem extremely active.

WOMAN 1: I've become impatient lately.

[*The* MAN *crosses from the downstage right tunnel to the opposite tunnel.*]

I'm eager to get going. There's been a long period of nothing, nothing at all. Now I'm really on the move.

WAITER: Well that's good, I would think.

[*Pause.*]

WOMAN 1: I would like you to feature.

[*Pause.*]

WAITER: There are plenty of things we could do together.

WOMAN 1: However there are some things I wouldn't want to do.

WAITER: And what might those be?

[*The* MAN *joins the* WOMEN *upstage.*]

WOMAN 1: There would be things. I can't be specific now. It was just a casual comment in passing.

WAITER: Oh. And likewise that you may do which I wouldn't, to be perfectly honest.

[*Pause.*]

WOMAN 1: Of course.

[*The* WAITER *leaves with his jug and there is silence.*]

THE WOMAN IN THE BLACK SEQUIN DRESS ARRIVES AT THE NIGHTCLUB

ENTRANCE 5 – THE CUP AND SAUCER

The MAN *walks towards upstage centre.* WOMAN 1 *goes to him and nestles her head onto his shoulder. He puts his arm around her.* WOMAN 4 *begins to move forward with her left arm out a little. The* MAN *takes her hand lightly and the three of them walk forward along the centre path.* WOMAN 3 *is deep in thought.* WOMAN 2 *stands still at the back, watching the others. As they walk forward, we hear the following text (voice over). Finally the text stops,* WOMAN 4 *turns and falls,* WOMAN 1 *slips to the floor.*

VOICE [*voice over*]: Over the grass over the washing machine over the cut up apple. Over the raw edges over the babies' nappies over the kisses over the past over the sink the bedroom, my mouth. Crunch crunch my feet land, it sinks under the floor, I push it down, my body travels up in a vertical line so I'm not looking down at the broken cutlery crockery. Knives and forks all going soft turning to liquid. Along the ironing board, the suitcases the tea towels out to the end of the pier. My table is over there, I'm doing well I'm half way there. Did I leave the TV on, was it on, something on? The kettle the gas stove, have I left my keys behind, will I be able to get back into the house, do I care if I do or if I don't? The grass is harsh and springy, cooch grass which grew over dry earth miraculously thick. My feet are sinking, I'm walking in a swimming pool. The children are asleep, they won't wake up. I'll just turn and check the distance,

check behind, is someone watching is someone behind me. I'll
check ...
  [WOMAN 4 *continues to walk a little then turns and falls.*]

FANTASY CONVERSATION WITH THE WOMAN IN THE BLACK SEQUIN DRESS

CONFUCIUS SAYS

We hear music. The WAITER *sets up a table and chairs downstage right. The* MAN *moves off to get a drink.* WOMAN 1 *and* WOMAN 4 *get up.* WOMAN 4 *goes and sits at the table. The* MAN *moves across to the table and stands stage right of it as* WOMAN 2 *moves to the table and sits on the upstage chair.* WOMAN 1 *moves upstage left and watches them from a distance. Throughout the scene the* WAITER *serves drinks. The feeling is flirtatious and they are having fun.*

MAN: May I join you.
WOMAN 4: Join me?
MAN: Yes.
WOMAN 1: I almost said, what, in holy matrimony?
MAN: Well, if you like. I'm not averse.
  [WOMAN 3 *goes and sits at the table on the left chair,*
  WOMEN 2, 3 *and* 4 *frequently giggle.*]
WOMAN 1: But actually I'm not averse either.
WOMAN 3: But perhaps we should get to know each other.
  [WOMAN 4 *slides low in her seat.*]
MAN: Yes of course.
  [*He looks at the chair situation.*]
  Perhaps I could sit ...
  [*Pause.*]
  ... on your chair while you sit on me.
WOMAN 4: We could.
  [WOMAN 2 *gets up and sits on the right chair.*]
MAN: I'd be happy to do that, to sit on a chair already warm. I'd like
  that very much indeed.
WOMAN 1: Well let's.

[WOMAN 1 *walks to the table and sits on the upstage right chair.* WOMAN 2 *gets up, the* MAN *sits on her chair and she sits on him. He feels the warmth of the chair.*]

MAN: Ah very nice. Warmth. Your warmth entering through the material of my trousers, then my underpants, to my skin, into my flesh.

WOMAN 4: Into your depths.

MAN: Into my depths.

[WOMAN 1 *looks knowingly at the other* WOMEN.]

WOMAN 3: The depths of your being.

[*They giggle. All continue to drink.* WOMAN 4 *turns to the audience.*]

WOMAN 4: Confucius says everything flows on like a river without pause day and night.

[*They drink and smile.*]

WOMAN 1: I've been watching the dance floor. It's extraordinary what comes up.

MAN: It's like water.

[*Pause.*]

You look like a queen sitting there in your lovely lovely sequin dress.

WOMAN 3: Do I?

[WOMAN 3 *gets up with her glass and dances by herself, aware of the* WAITER.]

MAN: A queen with an interesting brow behind which sit many thoughts, a mystery for me to untangle.

WOMAN 1: That's my job.

MAN: But I could stand by and be handy if you needed me.

WOMAN 3: Perhaps we could go for a swim on the dance floor.

MAN: With pleasure.

FANTASY DANCE 3: PLEASURE

WOMAN 2 *gets up and gradually begins dancing with the* MAN. *The* WAITER *watches them and* WOMAN 3. WOMAN 1 *speaks the following text as the others begin to dance. The* WAITER *takes the glass from* WOMAN 3 *and dances with her.* WOMAN 1 *is*

THE BLACK SEQUIN DRESS

BY JENNY KEMP

CAST

WOMAN 1	**Margaret Mills**
WOMAN 2	**Helen Herbertson**
WOMAN 3	**Natasha Herbert**
WOMAN 4	**Mary Sitarenos**
MAN	**Ian Scott**
WAITER	**Greg Stone**
GIRL'S VOICE	**Romanie Harper**

PRODUCTION

DIRECTOR	**Jenny Kemp**
COMPOSER	**Elizabeth Drake**
DESIGNER	**Jacqueline Everitt**
LIGHTING DESIGNER	**Ben Cobham**
CHOREOGRAPHY	**Jenny Kemp**
	Helen Herbertson
FILM MAKER	**Cassandra Tyler**
CAMERA	**Jesse Little Doring**
MUSICIANS	**Binneas String Quartet,**
	Jeremy Cook, Judy Pile,
	Danny Simcic,
	Jamie Southall
STAGE MANAGER	**Armando Licul**
ASSISTANT STAGE MANAGER	**Rod Scanlon**
PRODUCTION MANAGER	**Linda Aitken, Lachie A'Vard**
THEATRE TECHNICIAN	**Raymond Stepp**
SOUND OPERATOR	**Peter Eades**
WARDROBE CO-ORDINATOR	**Laura Doheny**
WORKSHOP SUPERVISOR	**Colin Orchard**
SCENIC ARTIST	**Marie Orchard**
SET CONSTRUCTION	**Playbox Workshop**
COVER IMAGE	**Paul Delvaux**

The Black Sequin Dress season at the Adelaide Festival and the Canberra Theatre Centre has been made possible with the assistance of Playing Australia. *The Black Sequin Dress* was commissioned by the 1996 Telstra Adelaide Festival.

PLAYING
AUSTRALIA

SPECIAL THANKS

Alexander Theatre, Austral Services Group, Barrisol Stretch Ceilings, Melanie Beddie, Margaret Cameron, Tom Considine, Julie Forsythe, Tammy McCarthy, Richard Murphet, Merfyn Owen, M. Maloney, Freya Matthews, Rob Meldrum, Ailsa Piper, Public Transport Corporation, Puffing Billy Railway, Michel Rowe and David Tredinnick; Film: Al, Daniel, Danny Darman of Darman Construction Divers, Dr Void, Flora, Henda, Jeff, Johnathon, Kerry Lee, Ruth, Simon and Tom.

Playbox is grateful for the support provided by Dolphin for the production of *The Black Sequin Dress*.

A woman in a black sequin dress leaves the children for the evening and goes to a nightclub. The play begins. The woman arrives at the nightclub. She walks across the shiny floor. In a moment of indecision she glances back, slips and falls. The waiter helps her up, walks her to a table and gets her a drink. The premise that any ordinary action has extraordinary resonances is explored. The nightclub becomes the underworld and falling synonymous with her psychic state. We watch as memory, desire, dream, fantasy and myth serve to animate the descent into the underworld and her subsequent ascent.

The production of *The Black Sequin Dress* derives inspiration from the paintings of surrealist artist Paul Delvaux.

"as you walk down the street into a nightclub you see the (real) world but feel aware of an inner world. The work attempts a dialogue with this disjunction.
An investigation into the psyche and its ability to function creatively."

"... we gain breadth of soul and wider horizons through vertical descent, through the inwardness of the image. Its puzzling peculiarity draws us down and in. The art of memory is an art of time, as work with memory always is. Unlike spiritual space travel that goes farther and farther `out', with freaking and peaking, highs and speed, the deepening of psychological space increases through slowness. The alchemists spoke of patience as a first quality of soul and considered soul-making the longest journey, a *via longissima*."

James Hillman
Falling Apart
from *Re-visioning Psychology*

JENNY KEMP
PLAYWRIGHT / DIRECTOR

Over the past decade Jenny has worked both as a director and a writer. As a playwright/director her work dates back to the early 80's (Stasis Group at The Pram Factory) with *The Point Isn't to Tell You*, *Sheila Alone* and *Jealousy* which toured to the Adelaide Festival of Australian Drama in 1979. She went on to adapt and direct D.M. Thomas' *The White Hotel* (Grant Street) and in the mid 80's wrote and directed *Good Night Sweet Dreams* (Anthill). In the late 1980's Jenny wrote and co-directed with Elizabeth Drake *Call of the Wild* for the Melbourne International Festival of the Arts and Belvoir St Theatre. In 1993 she wrote and directed *Remember* at the Gasworks. Jenny also worked in collaboration with Margaret Cameron on the original production of *Things Calypso Wanted to Say*. As a director, Jenny has worked with companies such as the Melbourne Theatre Company (*The Island, The Game of Love and Chance, Family Running for Mr Whippy*), the State Theatre Company of South Australia (*Big and Little*), The Mill (*Medea*) and The Pram Factory (*Peer Gynt* and *Antony and Cleopatra*). She also teaches and directs regularly at the Victorian College of the Arts School of Drama, directing a wide range of plays by playwrights such as Tennessee Williams, Botho Strauss, Chekhov, Racine, Fassbinder, Peter Gems and Caryl Churchill.

BEN COBHAM
LIGHTING DESIGNER

On Ben's twelfth birthday, his parents blessed him with 15 amp power to the garage. It was here that his first creations with light began, for his own backyard theatre shows. By sixteen, Ben was touring with Tasdance, One Extra and Dance North. Since then, having completed his Diploma of Dramatic Arts/Production at the Victorian College of the Arts, he has been prolific as a freelance lighting designer, mechanist and production manager, nationally and internationally. Ben recently had the opportunity to work for the Melbourne Theatre Company, Victoria State Opera and The Australian Ballet, all in one production of *Romeo and Juliet* at the State Theatre. His major interest is designing for visually based theatre, including most recently, Circus Oz, Danceworks and Recharge Theatre. Ben has also designed for music groups such as My Friend the Chocolate Cake, outdoor community spectaculars including the Mount Gambier Blue Lake Festival and the opening of the Renoir exhibition at the National Gallery of Victoria. Ben is currently interested in architectural interior lighting and bringing a theatrical influence to corporate events.

ELIZABETH DRAKE
COMPOSER

Elizabeth works as both a composer and as an artist who makes her own work. She is Artistic Director of The Spoken Opera Company currently with a project grant from the Hybrid Arts Board of the Australia Council. Works include *...And That is Very Interesting, Voices 2, Actual and Imaginary Undergrounds* and *Bloom*. She was a collective member of the Australian Performing Group and toured extensively with *Falling in Love Again* as a duo with Jan Cornall. She has composed music for numerous films and theatre productions, receiving an Australian Guild of Screen Composers Award for her work on the feature film *Breathing Underwater*. Elizabeth also received an AFI award nomination for Best Sound on an Experimental Film for *My Life Without Steve*. Elizabeth collaborated on *Call of the Wild* by Jenny Kemp and produced the work for radio on ABC-FM's 'The Listening Room'. Her work *Voices 2* was short listed in the national Sound Art competition of 'The Listening Room'.

Cultural and Cultural Oasis... Healthy Homemade food in a wonderful atmosphere...

The Malthouse Café has fresh muffins, bountiful lunch rolls, tasty frittatas, pies and salads, healthy soups and tempting daily specials. And of course, we make sublime coffee and cakes (the tira mi su is truly indulgent!)

Or relax with a beer or wine in our courtyard.

We're open from 8am weekdays and from midday on weekends.

malthouse café

113 sturt street south melbourne 3205 telephone 96 85 51 05

JACQUELINE EVERITT
DESIGNER

Jacqui has designed sets and costumes for productions by Playbox, La Mama, Anthill, The Church Theatre and the Melbourne Theatre Company. For Chamber Made Opera she designed *The Heiress, Recital, The Cars That Ate Paris, Lacuna* and costume for *Medea* and *Sweet Death*. Most recently for Chamber Made she designed Robert Ashley's *Improvement: Don Leaves Linda* produced for the Melbourne International Festival of the Arts. Other credits include *Seventy Scenes of Halloween* by Jeffrey Jones, *The Glass Mermaid* by Tobsha Learner, Jenny Kemp's *Call of the Wild* and *Dreams* directed by Lynne Maree Milburn.

NATASHA HERBERT
ACTOR

A 1991 graduate of the Victorian College of the Arts, Natasha first appeared for Playbox in the 1992 production of Tobsha Learner's *Wolf*. Later for Playbox she also appeared in *Love Child* (1993) and *Honour* (1995) both by Joanna Murray-Smith. Her work for the Melbourne Theatre Company includes *Hysteria, I Hate Hamlet, I'm Not Rappaport* and in their series of one act plays *Shorts*. Other theatre work includes Sam Sejavka's *In Angel Gear, The Misanthrope* at Napier Street Theatre, *Matilda* for New England Theatre Company and *Desirelines*, by Michael Gurr, for the Melbourne Festival. Natasha's television credits include *Newlyweds, Blue Heelers* and ABC-TV's acclaimed production of *The Damnation of Harvey McHugh*.

HELEN HERBERTSON
CHOREOGRAPHER / ACTOR

Performer, teacher and choreographer, Helen is currently Artistic Director of the Melbourne based Danceworks. In her seven years with the company, Helen has choreographed fourteen new works. Highlights include a Green Room Award for Best Production *No Strings Attached* in 1991, the ABC Radio National Fringe Award for Movement in 1994 with *Physical Business* and most recently the spectacular Danceworks outdoor presentation for the Melbourne International Festival of the Arts, *Vagabonds* and *High Flyers*. 1995 saw Helen as Visiting Fellow/Artist in Residence at the Dance Department, Faculty of Visual and Performing Arts, University of Western Sydney. In 1994 she was awarded three months at the Paris Studio through a Travel Study Grant from the Australia Council. Plans for 1996 include choreographing and performing in a new work to be premiered at the Green Mill Dance Project in July which will continue Helen's association with Jenny Kemp.

ARMANDO LICUL
STAGE MANAGER

Armando has been working with Playbox since The Malthouse premiere season on productions including *Wolf* (Tobsha Learner), *Sex Diary of an Infidel* (Michael Gurr), *The Temple* (Louis Nowra) and *Falling From Grace* (Hannie Rayson). Before that he worked for the Melbourne Theatre Company and the State Theatre Company of South Australia. He has toured extensively with Harvest Theatre Company as Stage Manager and Lighting Designer and with the Victorian Arts Council as Stage Manager. Most recently he stage managed the Playbox productions of Nick Enright's *Good Works* and *The Head of Mary* which toured to Japan.

MARGARET MILLS
ACTOR

Margaret last appeared for Playbox in *All Souls* (Daniel Keene) in 1995 and has worked with Jenny Kemp in *Remember* (Gasworks) and *Call of the Wild* (The Church, Belvoir St Theatre). Other credits include *Angels in America* Parts I and II and *Lady Windermere's Fan* for the Melbourne Theatre Company; *Ship of Fools* (Andrew Bovell), *A Thousand and One Nights* and *Geography* (Ian Scott) all co-written with Whistling in the Theatre; *The Girl I Love* and *Never Let Me Go* co-written with Maud Davey and Melissa Reeves for Short Arms, Long Pockets; *As Time Goes By* by Lyndal Jones; *Bending the Willow* (Don Asker) at the Victorian Arts Centre Studio; *The History of Water* by Noelle Janaczewska; *Song of Songs* with Robert Draffin; and *The Malady of Death, Closing Time* (Scott Taylor) and *Somewhere In Here Are Henry and Louisa* (Ian Scott) at La Mama. Margaret's television credits include *A Country Practice* and *Blue Heelers*.

IAN SCOTT
ACTOR

Ian has worked extensively in theatre, television and film. For Playbox, Ian first performed in *Britannicus* (1982). More recently he played Gloucester in *King Lear* which toured to Tokyo, Nagoya, Seoul, Perth and Canberra (1993/94) and last year in Sue Ingleton's *The Passion and its deep connection with lemon delicious pudding*. He has been involved with La Mama Theatre over a period of ten years in the capacity of writer, director and actor including a writer's residency in 1986. He appeared for the Church Theatre in *Dance in the Ashes*, Ernie Gray's adaptations of *Don Quixote* and *Treasure Island* and *This is the Way the World Ends* by Graham Shiells. Ian performed in numerous Anthill productions, including the premiere and return season of *The Imaginary Invalid* which also toured to the Adelaide Festival, in Bulghakov's *Molière*, for the Melbourne Spoleto Festival, *Waiting for Godot, Peer Gynt, Endgame, The Crimson Island* and the one-person show *Strategy for Two Hams*. He was engaged by the Melbourne Theatre Company for *Hedda Gabler, Rivers of China* (Alma De Groen) and *The Marriage of Figaro*, a joint production with Anthill and by Theatreworks for *Max, Popular Front, Storming St Kilda by Tram* (Paul Davies), *The Idiot* and *Rigoletto*.

PLAYBOX AND Q THEATRE PRESENT

GARY'S HOUSE

DEBRA OSWALD

A comic tale of born losers seeking their share
of the Australian dream.

MARY SITARENOS
ACTOR

Mary is an actor who has worked professionally for 15 years in both alternative and mainstream theatre, film and television. Some of her theatre credits include Tes Lyssiotis' *The Forty Lounge Cafe* and Tom Lindstrom's *Heroic Measures* (Playbox); *Too Young for Ghosts* (Janis Balodis) and *Les Liaisons Dangereuses* (Melbourne Theatre Company); Jean-Pierre Mignon's Chekhov Trilogy (Anthill); and *Blood Moon* (Tes Lyssiotis), *Song of Songs* (Robert Draffin), *Pericles* and *The Idiot* (Theatreworks). She performed in and co-wrote with composer Richard Vella the contemporary opera *Last Supper*. It toured Japan in 1995 and had seasons in Sydney (1993), Melbourne (1994) and goes to Tasmania in April this year. For the Melbourne Festival she appeared in Paul Carter, David Chesworth and Ariette Taylor's *Sabat Jesus* (Playbox 1990) and Luke Devenish and Ariette Taylor's *Disturbing the Dust* (Playbox 1994). Mary's previous work with Jenny Kemp includes *The White Hotel* and *Good Night Sweet Dreams*.

GREG STONE
ACTOR

Greg graduated from NIDA in 1983 and since then has worked extensively in theatre and television. His theatre work includes *Manning Clark's History of Australia – The Musical* (Tim Robertson, John Romeril and Don Watson), Therese Radic's *The Emperor Regrets* and *Good Works* by Nick Enright (Playbox), *All the Black Dogs* (Marilyn Allen) and Jim McNeil's *Old Familiar Juice* (Griffin Theatre Company), *Are You Lonesome Tonight?* by Pamela van Amstel (Western Australian Theatre Company), *Angels in America*, *Assassins* and *Lady Windermere's Fan* (Melbourne Theatre Company) and *Summer Rain* by Terence Clarke and Nick Enright (Sydney Theatre Company). Television credits include *A Country Practice*, *Rafferty's Rules*, *GP*, *The Man From Snowy River*, *Phoenix*, *Blue Heelers* and *Janus*. Greg has also worked as a musical director and composer on various productions and he spent two years as the lead singer with The Melody Lords. Most recently he appeared for Playbox in their production of *The Head of Mary* which toured to Japan.

NATIONAL THEATRE
Dance Classes

ADULT CLASSES
Get fit and have fun in a friendly, relaxed atmosphere. Beginners to experienced. Classical Ballet, Jazz, Tap.

CHILDREN'S CLASSES
R.A.D., Classical Ballet, A.I.C.D., Jazz, Tap. Dance Play for the very young.

DIPLOMA OF ARTS
Full-time dance training. (2 year course)

NATIONAL THEATRE BALLET SCHOOL
Cnr. Barkly & Carlisle Streets, St Kilda
For further information phone (03) 9534 0224

ARTISTIC DIRECTOR: MARILYN JONES O.B.E.
ADMINISTRATIVE DIRECTOR: JOANNE ADDERLEY

NATIONAL THEATRE
Drama School

THREE-YEAR PROFESSIONAL ACTING COURSE (EVENING CLASSES)
Admission limited and subject to individual interviews

ONE-YEAR ACTING AND MOVEMENT COURSE FOR SINGERS
Admission by audition and interview

DRAMA WORKSHOPS FOR YOUNG PEOPLE
9-18 & 18-20 years

NATIONAL THEATRE DRAMA SCHOOL
Cnr. Barkly & Carlisle Streets, St Kilda
For further information phone (03) 9534 0223

FOR PROSPECTUS AND APPLICATION FORM SEND SELF-ADDRESSED STAMPED ENVELOPE TO THE SECRETARY JILLIAN IRVINE, PO BOX 1173, ST KILDA SOUTH 3182
DIRECTOR: JOAN HARRIS A.M.

CANBERRA THEATRE CENTRE

ACKNOWLEDGEMENT
The Canberra Theatre Centre is administered by the
Canberra Theatre Trust which recives financial
assistance from the ACT Government through the
ACT Government's Minister for the Arts.

CANBERRA THEATRE TRUST
Chairman: Ian Meikle
Trustees: Anthony Hayward (Deputy Chairman),
Don Aitkin, Monica Barone Peter Guild, Sue Hamilton,
Kate Nockels, Inge Rumble. Richard Thorp

ADMINISTRATION
P.O. Box 226 Civic Square Canberra 2608
Ph: (06) 243 5711, Fax: (06) 243 5721

BOOKINGS at Canberra Ticketing
Ph: (06) 257 1077 or 1800 802 025

PLAYBOX THEATRE CENTRE OF MONASH UNIVERSITY

Aubrey Mellor
ARTISTIC DIRECTOR
Jill Smith
GENERAL MANAGER

Malcolm Robertson
LITERARY MANAGER
Tania Leong
ARTISTIC CO-ORDINATOR

Sarah Masters
ADMINISTRATOR
Jane Adair, Ingrid Nielsen
ADMINISTRATIVE ASSISTANT

Simon Bogle
MARKETING MANAGER
Simone Lourey
PUBLICIST
Christine Lucas-Pannam
Margaret Steven
EDUCATION OFFICER

Linda Aitken
PRODUCTION MANAGER
Laura Doheny
WARDROBE CO-ORDINATOR
Colin Orchard
WORKSHOP SUPERVISOR
Stuart McKenzie
THEATRE TECHNICIAN

THE C.U.B. MALTHOUSE

When you've got the tradition,
the pride and the spirit it shows
in everything you do

Carlton. One of the world's great brewers.
CUB proudly supporting Playbox Theatre Company.

remembering pleasure. WOMAN 4 *remains at the table and turns to looks out over the audience, then gets up and dances alone.* WOMAN 1 *gradually dances also – along the back centre path.*

WOMAN 1: Pleasure, ple, sure, please your. Ple shore by the shore. Pleasure by the beach. You're sure of pleasure by the shore. Pleasant pleasure, sinking, soft, sure, satisfying, pleasure. Please let me have pleasure. Please Peter let me have some pleasure. Please Janet let me have some pleasure. We're sure to have some pleasure by the shore. Sure. Given the dance floor is made of sea, it could be that we are able to have pleasure right here. Sure, we could, we could, we will dance on the shore for our pleasure.

THE WOMAN IN THE BLACK SEQUIN DRESS ARRIVES AT THE NIGHTCLUB

ENTRANCE 6 – PLEASURE

WOMAN 1 *walks to centre front as she speaks the following text. During this sequence the* WAITER *clears away the table and chairs.*

WOMAN 1: She relaxed as she entered through the small chink that suddenly appeared. She slid immediately straight through and did not look back, she sighed and released forward into the realm where ah, where ah, ah at last she was, she could be. Her arms were, her legs were, here lips were, yes she was wholly there. The pleasure, her pleasure, a pleasure, his pleasure, their pleasure, your pleasure, my pleasure, our pleasure, pleasure's pleasure.
[WOMAN 1 *stops and looks out to the audience.* WOMAN 3 *arrives and stands, smoking, at the right exit.*]
The stage seems a long way from the audience. There's a bit of a gulf between us. We'll have to project well. [*She raises her voice.*] Project well! [*Trying it out.*] And they sailed away for a year and a day to the land where the ...!
[*She walks off out the upstage right tunnel, reciting.*]

25

Is he pleasing her, is she pleasing him, they want to please each other and they want to be pleased.

FANTASY CONVERSATION WITH THE WOMAN IN THE BLACK SEQUIN DRESS

THE DARK MAN FROM THE SHADOWS

The WAITER, *with hat and jacket, arrives at the right exit and lights up a cigarette.* WOMAN 4 *sits on the train (facade off), next to the skeleton, watching the dance floor and smiling as it passes slowly by from right to left. There is a blackboard on the train with "les planets" written on it.*

WOMAN 3: Ah the dark man from the shadows is here.
WAITER: Yes, here I am.
WOMAN 3: Well I'm so pleased to meet you. Tell me what's your name and what are you like, and what do you think of me?
WAITER: My name is Tom. And I like you. And I think you're gorgeous.
WOMAN 3: Goodness you are so direct in your speech. How interesting.
WAITER: There's more to me than meets the eye.
WOMAN 3: I'm sure.
    [*Pause.*]
    I'd hoped there would be.
    [*Pause.*]
    Do you ever get frightened?
WAITER: Perhaps I could be of you.
WOMAN 3: I do have dark thoughts at times.
    [*Pause. Smiles.*]
    But I'm light and bright tonight. I'm in a sparkling mood.
    [WOMAN 2 *walks to the earth with the box. She stands looking at box. She has a naked top and bottom. Satin skirt.*]
WAITER: I would say of the dangerous kind.
WOMAN 3: You're right.
WAITER: How about a drink, and something to eat?
    [*The train disappears. We hear the river.*]

26

MYTH 4: CROSSING THE RIVER STYX – OPENING THE BOX

We see WOMAN 1 *at the small window. On the sill is a model of the Earth and the phases of the Moon. Her head is down on the sill. She is asleep.* WOMAN 2 *is standing on the earth with a naked top and black satin skirt. She is holding the box. She stands silently for some time then she opens the box. We hear gushing water. She is wrapped in a dense cloud of drowsiness and falls slowly to the ground, in a Stygian sleep.*

SEQUENCE C: THE UNDERWORLD / DOING THE WORK

NIGHTMARE 4

WOMAN 1 *wakes up suddenly and lifts her head from the sill at the window.*

WOMAN 1: What's that! What was that scream? I thought I heard a scream.
[*She looks behind her. She is shaking.*]
I need a drink of water. I think I fell, or someone fell.
[*Pause.*]
I need some water.

COUNTRY WALK 3: EXPANSE OF WATER

We see a projected image/film of the WOMAN, *swimming naked underwater (2 min). The* MAN *enters and walks slowly from the upstage right tunnel towards the upstage end of the earth. He watches* WOMAN 2. *He calls softly, "Help me I'm drowning." He is wearing small horns. The text is spoken by* WOMAN 4 *(offstage microphone).*

WOMAN 4: Undine lowers the upper part of her body and stretches her bare arms out in front of her. Her head is practically hidden as it lies poised in between her upper arms. There is a large expanse of water stretching in front of her. Man enters. Her knees bend and all the muscles in her legs flex as she leaves the bank and disappears inside the surface of the water. Her wet head reappears at a surprising distance from the shore. The tension in her shoulders works its way into the body of the water as she pushes and strokes her way through its heavy mass. As she swims she alternates her gaze from across the surface of the water, down through the dark water into the density of its substance where she can see the dark depth filled, totally filled with her own imagination. Eventually as her shoulders open the doorway into her body she finally relaxes and swims with her own rhythm as if she were made for water, her mouth slightly sucking in the water and blowing it out. The man begins to call out more loudly. She manages to swim fluently across the surface of the large lake as she feels she really needs to get to the other side if she is to survive.

MYTH 5: CROSSING THE RIVER STYX – HELP ME I'M DROWNING

We hear water gushing and the horned MAN, *now in a horrifying yet distant voice, screams the following as he remains poised over her unconscious body.*

MAN: Help me! Please help me! Please help me into the boat please save me, I'm drowning!
   [*The following action occurs simultaneously.* WOMAN 1, *with a ball held on her palm, walks from the right exit across to the left exit, along the centre tunnel and then along the back tunnel. She stops in her tracks when she is upstage left, facing the tunnel entrance.* WOMAN 3 *hurries along the tunnels with loaves and coin.* WOMAN 4 *carries the large box. She is exhausted and continually checks behind her as she struggles on. The* WOMEN *walk on, not allowing themselves to be affected by the call for help.*]

FANTASY CONVERSATION WITH THE WOMAN IN THE BLACK SEQUIN DRESS

FLYING FISH

The WAITER *enters from the left tunnel and stands opposite* WOMAN 1. *We see the planet Earth and the Moon at the small window. A* WITCH, *looking ghostly and grey, with long hair like cobwebs, stands in the right exit with an owl perched on her wrist. We can see the body above the left exit.*

WAITER: Something about you gives me hope, so I've come up to introduce myself. Jack, Jonathan, Jack. I can imagine dancing with you, there would be palm trees, moonlight, flying fish in the air. Perhaps I would have horns growing out of my head.
  [*The* MAN *with the horns is lying over* WOMAN 2.]
WOMAN 1: I love the sea. I'm a deep sea diver. I float down like a sinker, straight to the bottom. No wonder you thought of flying fish, it's almost true.
WAITER: We could if you like, now, dance.

FANTASY DANCE 4: THE CARNIVALE

A wild group dances across the stage from the left exit to the right exit. WOMAN 3 *dances with the skeleton.* WOMAN 2, *in a skeleton mask, dances erotically with the dummy. The* WAITER *then arrives and picks her up onto his shoulders.* WOMAN 4 *is the witch; she walks sideways through the group. The* MAN *is drunken and lewd with a mask.* WOMAN 1 *stands with her ball, mouth ajar, and watches.*

WOMAN 1 *teeters, drops the ball and falls very slowly. This text should be spoken softly and slowly (on offstage microphone) by* WOMAN 4, *as* WOMAN 1 *falls. After falling,* WOMAN 1 *crawls her way off down the upstage left tunnel.* WOMAN 3 *then crawls on from the upstage right tunnel and over to the earth, where she collapses exhausted. An enormous tree, roots first, lowers over* WOMAN 3. *She appears buried.*

WOMEN'S VOICES [*voice-over*]: Suddenly there is black space and the mountain is flying past. I'm crying my tears are shooting out and falling on my shirt front. I'm a mess. I'm falling down right down as if from a higher rise building, as if I've wilfully jumped, as if I want to fall forever. The inside stone of the mountain, wet walls, falling upside down to land in a crash where everything should completely pulverise. But unfortunately it seems your eyes open and you notice that you can move your legs.

   [*Her body lands. She then begins to lift her head and move into the crawl off.*]

You sit up your head slowly veers backwards, your eyes lift and you see it again, the long craggy path. Feel the wet walls, look an inch in front of your nose if you want to, lie still and stare at the wall forever, in the dark, quite still near the rock wall,

   [WOMAN 3 *crawls on.*]

... listen to the density of the rock, stay right here and sleep for a hundred years, if you want to.

   [WOMAN 3 *lies still.*]

THE WOMAN IN THE BLACK SEQUIN DRESS ARRIVES AT THE NIGHTCLUB

ENTRANCE 7 – SHE WALKS TO HER TABLE

We hear music. The WAITER *enters and stands between the left tunnel.* WOMAN 4 *enters from the upstage left tunnel (upstage of rails), as the* MAN *enters from the downstage left tunnel, he sits on the left chair with his glass.* WOMAN 4 *enters and pauses upstage centre. The* WAITER *begins to speak the following text at this moment and continues as she walks forward along the centre path. He does not look at her.* WOMAN 3 *remains on the earth under the tree.*

WAITER: The woman who is now not so young, more middle aged, of an age which confuses the onlooker, this woman dressed smartly in a glamorous, svelte black sequin dress walks into the nightclub her eyes are held, she has not had a drink, she has not been to a nightclub for years. Almost immediately one is aware of the precariousness of her long journey from door to table. First there is the choice of which table,
    [WOMAN 4 *stops for a moment.*]
... then there is the high sheen of the floor to traverse in her new dance shoes. But of course dance shoes were made to be partnered and at this stage there is no partner. She steps out feeling no doubt as if she is on an ice skating rink or indeed alternatively in an enormous desert through which she has to travel, without a drink. Her body is upright, perpendicular. Her face at present appears almost mask-like. Over one shoulder is slung small black bag, which no doubt holds lipstick, comb, perfume and cigarettes, if she is a smoker. She looks as if she could be a smoker or as if she has spent quite a deal of time inside. Her skin is very pale. Her eyes very dark even though they could be blue. She has identified the table and is travelling in that direction, which is to her left, she is veering left. At approximately half way from the door to the table something

occurs which upsets her progress. She glances back over her right shoulder and up to the balcony behind her, just glances as if she suddenly remembered to look or had been instructed at this point to turn and acknowledge a friend in the balcony, or perhaps a certain nervousness causes her to look back because she suspects she is being watched by someone.

[*The* WOMAN *does these actions but not necessarily as he says them.*]

At this moment she is thrown off balance, her left foot slips and loses its formerly secure contact with the high sheen floor and her body crumples, appears to cave in and land in a heap, quite a small heap in the centre of the nightclub. The heap is instantly quite still. In looking more closely one can see that the head is thrown backwards, one leg is stretched out while one is trapped beneath the body. Nothing happens immediately. Then the waiter hurries to her side addressing her sharply with the words, "Madam are you all right?"

[*The* WOMAN *stirs, looks up and around her and then proceeds to get up as if the* WAITER *were helping her.*]

She then responded, gave him a sign and then he proceeded to help her the rest of the way across the floor.

[*She then moves quite quickly towards the left chair. The* MAN, *at the moment she starts in his direction, anticipates her need, vacates the chair and moves downstage a few metres and stands by the wall with his drink. She sits in the chair and receives a drink from the* WAITER.]

Compared to the first half of her journey this second half now seemed over in only a few seconds.

[*He hands her a brandy from the shelf above.*]

... and very soon she was sitting drinking brandy with almost a trace of a smile on her lips.

[*She sits and orientates. She takes in the presence of the* MAN *and he her. They both maintain their feeling of aloneness, yet allow and remain open to each other's presence.*]

FANTASY CONVERSATION WITH THE WOMAN IN THE BLACK SEQUIN DRESS

DEAD BODY IN THE DESERT

This scene is with WOMAN 4 *and the* MAN. *They are both quite still.*

WOMAN 4: In the desert at night after a day that was so hot it should have burst into flames, no one could move. I sat so still I thought I was dead. My flesh was melting. We tried to keep the body where we could see it, but it was rotting, the stench was so great we had to refrigerate it. I didn't care we could all drop dead, I thought I will stay sitting here forever. It was no longer even him. I was tired. I didn't even remember how I got out of there, but one day I was in a car watching the desert going past out the window, the car was air conditioned and it was time to go back, so I was going back.
   [WOMAN 4 *stops talking. There is a pause. Perhaps she sobs.*] This is grief pouring out of me. You can watch. It will still happen whether you watch or not. I'll disintegrate, I'm ninety percent water you know.

MAN: I can see, you're a paradox, a glamorous paradox.

WOMAN 4: Well whatever you mean,
   [*She drops a glass.*]
   Ah you see I've smashed a glass, it's shattered.
   [*Pause.*]

MAN [*clears the glass up*]: Can I do anything to help?

WOMAN 4: You could pour me a glass of water.

MAN: What after all am I here for?
   [*He hands her water whilst watching her. Then he steps back towards his former position and stands still.*]

WOMAN 4: I don't know, what are you here for?

MAN [*embarks*]: From a certain distance I see you. [*Moves in a few steps.*] But the closer I get the greater your surface, you are no longer an outline a simple shape of hair and dress and shoes, you

34

are details, endless lines to be drawn. [*Moves closer.*] And when I go in further so much, more and more.

WOMAN 4: I have nothing to say. I have fallen over, and I haven't been able to get up because my legs don't work. I don't care about any of you any more. At last I don't care, the world has swallowed me up.

[*The* MAN *moves away from her back to his former position.*]

MAN: I am only a humble man, I have many imperfections. [*Looks at his hands.*] I've even got dirt under my finger nails.

[*Pause.*]

I could give you a rub on the neck, sponge your face put you to bed.

WOMAN 4: I'm tired. I need a rest.

MAN: Of course you do. I'll tuck you up in clean white sheets with a soft pillow.

WOMAN 4: With a warm drink and something to eat.

MAN: You can stay there as long as you like. These things take time.

WOMAN 4: I sacrificed it all everything inside this dress.

MAN: But I can see it perfectly well, you are luminous, only you can't see.

[*Pause.*]

Just think of yourself as a woman.

WOMAN 4: I do.

[*Pause.*]

Death. Do you know anything about it?

MAN: No, frankly, I don't. Oh, war yes, war death I do.

WOMAN 4: No not that kind.

MAN: The other, no.

WOMAN 4: I like you, you see, I feel like I can relax with you. Secure, I feel that, foreign as it may sound, to myself. Secure, the word cure right there inside it, see cure. And see. A clever word.

MAN: I've been too busy to have any real contact with death. Frankly I've been empire building, I'm a rich man.

WOMAN 4: And popular.

MAN: Yes.

WOMAN 4: How much do you like me?

MAN: I find you incredibly attractive and I'm moved, and that's rare.

WOMAN 4: You're attracted to a cesspool.

MAN: Well it doesn't look like that to me.

WOMAN 4: Just as well.

[*Pause.*]

Out in the desert I have a commitment to uphold and you're the one I choose to help me.

[*Pause.*]

Lucky you.

MAN: Lucky me. And what do I do exactly?

WOMAN 4: Well you start by hiring some camels, you'll need to spend some time acclimatising getting to know the ropes.

MAN: But I'm a business man.

WOMAN 4: I know, exactly, that's why you're the one, you see I need the business man for the otherside of the story.

MAN: Oh good I'm glad he'll prove useful. By the way he's damn good at hiring the right man for the job.

WOMAN 4: I know, but I'm doing the hiring.

MAN: Well let's proceed as if I'm the one and I've accepted the deal. What next?

WOMAN 4: You'll think I'm being bizarre, but I want you to collect a body for me, a dead body.

[*Pause.*]

MAN: Yes, then what?

WOMAN 4: Bring it back. I can't do it myself.

MAN: Why me?

WOMAN 4: I trust you, and this is a private affair.

MAN: It is?

WOMAN 4: It is.

MAN: You're quite serious aren't you.

WOMAN 4: Oh yes, deadly serious. What I like about you is you bite. You're biting aren't you.

MAN: What are you going to do with it when it's back?

WOMAN 4: I have to give it a proper burial.

[*Pause.*]

I don't actually feel that man is, like Adam up on the Sistine Chapel touched by the hand of God. He might just as well be a crow. Who cares he's only part of the story.

[*Silence.*]

MAN: Cheers!

WOMAN 4: He is certainly as good as a crow however. Or a magpie.

[*Pause.*]

MAN: Your dress fits you beautifully, as if it was poured around your body. You are luminescent as you sit there, with your strange smile, your red lips and your enigmatic eyes.

[*Pause.*]

WOMAN 4: Lovely wine. Dry and slightly harsh ... I like it a lot. You're massive in your intent, I can see that.

MAN: It's clearly your night go for it, I'm here for the taking.

[*She moves over, stands near him and sips her drink.*]

WOMAN 4: Reality is things, very small things, invisible things.

MAN: My imagination is moving into you. What a landscape I find I have to traverse.

WOMAN 4: It's out in the middle of the desert.

[*Pause.*]

MAN: Ah.

WOMAN 4 [*holds out her arm*]: Touch my arm. It's solid, it's real, it's not poetry, not imagination. It is concrete.

MAN: Yes. Are you asking me or telling me.

WOMAN 4: About my arm telling, about the desert asking.

MAN: You're serious.

WOMAN 4: Yes. Very, but I've got a sense of humour too.

MAN: Good.

[*Pause. Touches her arm.*]

I'll do it.

[*He stands still for a moment then departs by the left exit. There is a long pause. Everything is still terror is creeping in. The tree lifts from on top of* WOMAN 3 *and slowly disappears.*]

37

NIGHTMARE 5

WOMAN 4 *stands and fills with tension.* WOMAN 3 *sits upright as if she has just arrived up from the bottom of the earth and now gasps the air back in. She is in a state of terror. She slowly rises, goes to the wall for water. She drinks and then slowly turns, still clutching her glass to look behind her. At this moment the* MAN *enters, carrying the skeleton, from the downstage left tunnel opposite her.*

THE WOMAN IN THE BLACK SEQUIN DRESS ARRIVES AT THE NIGHTCLUB

ENTRANCE 8 – TERROR

The following actions occur simultaneously. WOMAN 1 *enters. She is naked with a bag over her shoulder and shoes on. She walks on slowly along the same central path.* WOMAN 2 *stands quite still at the window. The* MAN *proceeds slowly upstage, next to the wall, along the back, then down the other side and into the right exit. He does not look at the* WOMEN. WOMAN 3 *keeps her eyes on him and steps out of his way back onto the earth as he passes. After a while* WOMAN 4 *sits down then takes out her lipstick and mirror and does her face and hair to keep terror at bay. It is as if she is impatiently waiting for someone to return.*

WOMAN 1: Terrorise, terrorist, terrify, terrible, terrific terror. I feel terror, tremendously terrifying terror. I feel terrible. I feel terrified of this terror I feel. Don't terrorise me, you terrible thing. I will terrorise with my terror. I am a terrorist, a terrible terrorist so watch out. I am terrific at knowing about terror right on this edge of terror I stand, I look to the left, I look to the right, terror, no terror. I look straight ahead. I'm in trouble. What is terror?
   [*She stops. Her eyes shift to the left, then the right and back to centre.*]

The space between the left and the right, from my nose straight ahead to some terrible and unimaginable horizon. A landscape of terror, monstrous, empty. Tables and chairs and people all terribly normal right to the awful horizon. Step by step all alone, from left to right I look as my feet press on. Deserted in my terrible landscape, should I look back, turn my head? Which way? Through the right landscape or the left I wonder, to get to the back, to look at the something terrible which is bound to be, now at this moment, right behind me.

[*She stops. Her head turns to the left.*]

... it's gone, over my left shoulder, my head, it's looking back. Of course, of course, of course. Nothing but the shiny floor I've already stepped over. Well, I could have told you that you idiot. True, true, I knew that, just looked without thinking. Got to get the head back to the front now. Gently,

[*She turns her head back towards the front and a little to the right, just missing seeing the* MAN, *departing into the right exit.*]

... ah, in control. Gaze serenely detached, don't give a careless damn over the landscape, trees, grass, well how beautiful it all is. I wander on down the pleasant path, I hold it at bay,

[WOMAN 4 *stands tensely and glances around.*]

... it's wandered off terror, slipped off like a fish off to somewhere else to dart back whenever it pleases.

[*At this moment the target should finish its descent. She stops, turns and falls.*]

FANTASY CONVERSATION WITH THE WOMAN IN THE BLACK SEQUIN DRESS

WHAT'S THE TIME SIMON?

The MAN *appears from the upstage right tunnel. He is holding a tray with balls of minced steak stacked on it. He remains near the tunnel throughout the scene.* WOMAN 4 *begins to back downstage. She keeps moving backwards throughout the whole scene.*

WOMAN 4 [*moving backwards*]: What's the time Simon? Have we really got time for this drink?

MAN: Well yes of course we have, we planned it so we would.

WOMAN 4: I know, I know. I just thought we took rather a long time getting here. And now what with ordering then waiting for it to come ...

MAN: It will be fine. We'll be fine.

WOMAN 4: Do you think?

MAN: I would suspect I could die for you.

WOMAN 4: Would you? Would you die for me?

MAN: Die?

WOMAN 4: Yes die.

MAN: Well the answer right off the top of my head, standing here right in front of you. I would have to say the answer is yes.

[*Pause.* WOMAN 4 *stops. She is, even though she doesn't know it, right on the edge of the stage.*]

And I'm suprised I seem to mean it. I'll order some wine.

WOMAN 4: That's very pleasing news.

[*He leaves.* WOMAN 4 *steps backwards and falls off the stage and into the audience. There is a blackout. A large target is lowered into the space upstage and the* WITCH *stands by the target with a large steel stockpot.*]

RECIPE FOR COLD BORSCH SOUP

We hear the following text (voice over: WOMAN 4*) in blackout.*

WOMAN 4 [*voice over*]: 1 & half pounds of lean beef
  2 quarts of salted water
  3 sprigs of parsley
  2 leeks
  2 carrots
  1 bay leaf
  1 clove of garlic
  6 peppercorns
  1 pound of cooked beetroot diced
  Half a red cabbage, coarsely chopped
  2 potatoes
  2 onions
  Half a pound of mushrooms
  Half a pint of sour cream.

MEMORY: MEAT THROWING DREAM

As the lights come up we hear music and the WAITER *speaking the following text – as a running commentary.* WOMEN 1, 2, 3 *and* 4 *are standing naked with their backs to the audience. They all have several balls of minced meat in each hand. In front of* WOMAN 1 *there is a tray with a stack of the meatballs on it. The* WITCH *still stands by the target. The* WOMEN *all throw a ball of meat at the target, then another.* WOMAN 1 *picks up the tray and steps forward and throws another. The others all step forward and aim and throw also (but now without any meat). They advance towards the target, their aims getting better and better. There is a serious feeling at first but, as they continue, they become more and more celebratory. Finally, when they are quite close to the target,* WOMAN 1 *slams the meat in the centre on the bullseye, and then turns and raises her arms to the audience in celebration. She proceeds down the centre path towards the front, miming aiming and throwing bullseyes. She also mimes successful bow and arrow shoots. As she travels towards the front, the target flies slowly up and out. The* WITCH *turns and leaves by the upstage left tunnel.* WOMEN 2 *and* 4 *also leave by the upstage tunnels and* WOMAN 3 *goes back to the earth, reciting the following text to herself.* WOMAN 1 *stops centre front again, raises her arms, turns in a circle, then saunters off through the right exit, eye balling the audience as she goes.*

WAITER: The woman takes the piece of meat and immediately takes aim and throws it straight across the floor, straight as an arrow indeed as an arrow the meat flies from the determined hand through the space to land with a satisfying thwack right in the dead centre of the target – Bullseye! Straight as an arrow, it has landed as she knew, as her body knew, right on target. Again her arm levers back, all the muscles, tightening, lifting the bone of her forearm up and over her shoulder. Inside her hand is clutched a lump of meat, wet raw meat, minced meat, in a ball. Her eyes are narrowing, squinting and taking focus on something in the distance across the floor, across the earth, across the desert, across the open space, over the other side of the nightclub. Over the polished dance floor upon which several hours ago she slipped and fell, she now throws a lump of meat.

UNDINE'S VOICE – A KILOMETRE OF SOUND

A film of the desert appears. It is a 360 degree pan of the desert and horizon. Three or four rotations are made (2 mins). WOMAN 2 *is at the window with her mouth wide open in a Munch-like silent scream. The following text is spoken by* WOMAN 1 *(microphone offstage). The* WAITER *enters towards the end of the scene and stands still downstage left, towards the centre.*

WOMAN 1: The sound comes out of her body. It must have been coiled up inside her, a kilometre of sound, it would have ravaged her insides if it could with its violence, it wants to take everything with it and destroy it. But her body simply opens and empties itself into the volume of sound. Between the vowel and something like a consonant at the other end, it seems to travel with great volition without damaging anything on the way. Her body lets it out, wants it out, to scare away her own fear, she screams a bloody scream, to force everything out of her room, out of herself, her tongue her lips pull back and she screams her way back up out of her nightmare.
[*The film disappears. There is silence. We see* WOMAN 3 *sit up.*]

UNDINE'S STORY – DESIRE / MEMORY ENACTMENT

WOMAN 4 *speaks the following text (offstage microphone).* WOMAN 3 *relaxes, gets up and puts on her slip which is beside the earth. She takes a glass of water, drinks and yawns. She wanders around the room quite comfortable with herself and as if alone. The* WAITER *is still standing in the same spot. He is lost in his own reverie. She returns to the earth and sits on the downstage corner. At this moment the text starts. At times the* WAITER *and* WOMAN 3 *speak the lines simultaneously with* WOMAN 4. WOMAN 4 *continues to speak throughout, however, with only the usual pauses for the rhythm of the telling. There is a strong sexual feeling apparent between the* WAITER *and* WOMAN 3. *During the scene* WOMAN 3 *wanders around but the* WAITER *remains standing on the same spot.*

WOMAN 4'S VOICE: Below the belly button screams inside her, yet she cannot move. The sounds around her are acute the smells. Alone in the brick house Undine desires a man. At this moment Undine's egg moves along it's passage making it's presence felt in all sorts of ways. All sorts of details occur throughout the body of Undine. He knocks on her door, she goes and opens the door, she smiles and says ...

WOMAN 3 [*looking across at* WAITER]

& WOMAN 4'S VOICE [*simultaneously*]: Hello.

    [*The* WAITER *has just begun watching* WOMAN 3.]

WOMAN 4'S VOICE: She can hardly stand up now with her enormous egg travelling inside. He doesn't know, she knows he doesn't that there is an egg travelling inside her. He puts out his hand and speaks ...

WAITER

& WOMAN 4'S VOICE [*simultaneously*]: I'm sorry. It's so late and I haven't seen you for so many years.

    [*The* WAITER *pauses as the story rolls on, then speaks again.*]
Odd that now at this incongruous hour here I am.

WOMAN 3 [*with a slight smile*]

& WOMAN 4'S VOICE [*simultaneously*]: Well no. No a good time to call really.

WOMAN 4'S VOICE: She glances up at his eyes and notices their colour. He steps forward across the threshold, and she imagines him carrying a bride. But she steps back and then closes the door. Her face is soft today, there is no fight in her today because of her ovulation. She just stands there whereas normally she would make an effort and socially do something, so he stops too. He doesn't know she is full of desire, can he see it? She's not sure. She goes and sits down and turns to look at him and says –

[WOMAN 3 *walks around and to the centre, stretches and yawns.*]

WOMAN 3

& WOMAN 4'S VOICE [*simultaneously*]: How come you've come to visit me?

[WOMAN 3 *pauses.*]

I thought you didn't like me, all those years ago?

WOMAN 4'S VOICE: He smiles ...

[WAITER *pauses.*]

WAITER

& WOMAN 4'S VOICE [*simultaneously*]: Well yes it's true I was scared in a way. You ...

WOMAN 4'S VOICE: He stops ...

WAITER

& WOMAN 4'S VOICE [*simultaneously*]: Never mind ...

WOMAN 4'S VOICE: ... she says ...

[WOMAN 3 *pauses.*]

WOMAN 3

& WOMAN 4'S VOICE [*simultaneously*]: It's good to see you.

WOMAN 4'S VOICE: She wanted suddenly to touch him, she relaxed she didn't care now about the inappropriateness of anything. She could say whatever came into her head, she could let it all be. The room was now in three dimensions. She saw into the corners of the room ...

WAITER: Are you tired?

WOMAN 4'S VOICE: ... she saw the depth of space, she saw there was space between them and around them both. She stood up and stretched her arms above her head, and actually yawned.

[*She lies on the earth.*]

He asked if she was tired ...

WAITER: Are you tired ?

WOMAN 4'S VOICE: ... she said she was and she might go to bed if he didn't mind. He could sleep somewhere here if he liked. He said yes he would stay, he would sleep on her floor if she didn't mind.

WAITER: Yes I will stay.

[*Pause.*]

I'll sleep on your floor if you don't mind.

[*He remains standing on his spot.*]

SEQUENCE D: COMING BACK UP WITH THE CHILD

THE NIGHTCLUB RETURNS

Music snaps on loud. The WAITER *immediately begins setting up a table and two chairs in the downstage right corner, chairs first.* WOMAN 1 *and the* MAN *enter and sit. They are in a good mood. The* WAITER *brings the table, then a bottle and glasses. He fills their glasses then leaves the bottle with them. He sets up another table just outside the downstage left tunnel.* WOMAN 2 *enters, tentatively, from the upstage right tunnel. The* WAITER *gets her a table, pours her a drink, then leaves.* WOMAN 3 *leaves by the upstage right tunnel.*

FANTASY CONVERSATION WITH THE WOMAN IN THE BLACK SEQUIN DRESS

MEMORY – BALL IN GULLY

MAN: We call the weather on a night like tonight, memory.

WOMAN 1 [*turns*]: Oh. And who are we?

MAN: Of course if the weather changes, we then call it misery. But tonight it is memory.

    [*The* WOMAN *looks at him with curiosity. He smiles.*]

WOMAN 1: I remember lying at the bottom of a gully, a damp fern gully. I had gone to find my ball, but my leg got caught and I fell on my back. I knew there were leeches there but I had no desire to get up. I just lay there and wondered if my leg was broken.

    [*The* WAITER *delivers nibbles.*]

Eventually my father called, "Are you all right?" and I decided not to reply, to let him think I was dead. I finally heard his footsteps, I thought he'll get leeches in his socks, they'll suck his

45

blood. I stayed very quiet and he hunted and hunted calling my name.

[*Pause.*]

Then I didn't know what to do, I lost my courage. So I got up and started walking to the top of the gully. And when I was up I called out, "Dad, where are you?"

[*Pause.*]

And he called back, "Oh there you are"and just walked back up the hill as if nothing had happened.

[*Pause.*]

And then I had yet another secret I had to keep in my chest on top of all the others.

MAN: I would like to travel to the bottom of a gully with you. You could lie down there quite flat and heavy on the ground, and I believe I could pick you up and carry you right back up the hill. We could make it a long slow journey.

WOMAN 1: In all honesty I can imagine doing just that.

[*Pause.*]

I find it liberating to be able to tell someone what's on my mind don't you? I feel that if I give voice to something crouched up and silent inside then I can move on.

[*Pause while they drink and relax in good humour.* WOMAN 2 *stands as if to leave, but remains still.*]

A REAL CATASTROPHE – WOMAN FAINTS

WOMAN 2 *falls in a heap on the floor. The idea is that the audience thinks that she has really fainted. The* MAN *and* WOMAN 1 *look across and giggle slightly, they obviously think it's some kind of joke. Then they notice she is not moving and they get worried. At this point it should begin to look like the actors have come out of character as something is really wrong. They go across to check her, trying to look like this is not really happening or trying to make it look like part of the play. They attend to her but she still does not respond. They get really worried and, still trying to cover up from the audience, call the* STAGE MANAGER *to help them.* WOMAN 3 *comes running on from the right tunnel, her dress not fully on and trying not to be too noticable. They eventually carry*

46

her off. Meantime the train has nudged slightly on to the stage from the right tunnel and stopped. The STAGE MANAGER *is confused.*

FANTASY CONVERSATION WITH THE WOMAN IN THE BLACK SEQUIN DRESS

ON THE TRAIN – OVULATION

In the first compartment is an enormous ball. Then we see WOMAN 4 *sitting opposite the* WAITER. *They do not move from their seats. The second text, "I breathe", is spoken by* WOMAN 1 *(offstage microphone) simultaneously with the dialogue as the train crosses.* WOMAN 3 *enters from the left exit and sits on the downstage left chair.* WOMAN 2 *enters from the upstage right tunnel, walks downstage and stands just near the table. The* MAN *enters and stands on his upstage spot.*

WAITER: Shall I massage your neck? Loosen your clothes?

WOMAN 4: Yes. Reality is very small things.

WAITER: Your skin looks hot.

WOMAN 4: It's no wonder I'm ovulating, just here just behind my dress.
    [*Pause.*]
    And you are responding. It's only natural.

WAITER: Of course.

WOMAN 4: My breasts feel the pressure my nipples are pressing against my dress. My ovum is being forced along the fallopian tube, it will collide with the wall of my womb. It makes me feel helpless.

WAITER: Shall we lie down under the seat? I could help it along its path, I could soften the impact of the collision.
    [*The train disappears.*]

WOMAN 4: Yes we could.

47

I BREATHE AT LAST I BREATHE

Spoken simultaneously with above:

VOICE: I breathe at last I breathe, my body opens it breathes, we breathe, you and I together, immobilised action, action inside everywhere you you you are, oh you are I am, I am full, filling up, fill me up, yes you are all over me, I am everywhere, no arms legs body. But yes arms legs body face breath hair all I have everything I need right here with you, with you, you darling, you darling.

NIGHTMARE 6

We hear the "What's that" text as voice over as WOMAN 4 *enters with a glass of water and stands on the earth.*

WOMAN 3 [*voice over*]: What's that! What was that scream? I thought I heard a scream. I need a drink of water. I think I fell, or someone fell.
   [*Pause.*]
I need some water.

IT'S AS IF MY BODY HAS BEEN TAKEN APART

WOMAN 1, *in the day dress, stands embracing the* MAN *(the dummy) in the left exit and speaks the following text. A repeat of the AZB scenario is enacted here (see page 5), but several of the* WOMEN *have swapped positions. However, instead of leaving the stage, all remain on stage (after the ball goes off on the train).*

WOMAN 1: It's as if my body had been taken apart and put together again. One part separated from another, all floating, speeding off, as if bombed, shooting out into the darkness, the universe, and put together again. Again as if all this may have happened many times before. Something better this time, put together, by the force of the return flight, after the bombing which had just occurred. A shock which something in me knows all about. But now I don't. What could it be? a memory – which returned with an incredible force, fell, or was propelled from one area into another. Perhaps there was a kind of explosion in this area which set it free, or maybe just things changed ... [*The train disappears.*] ... then the shock was the new arrangement.

[WOMAN 3 *sits at the table.*]

Something completely different after all these years.

[*All on stage stand in stillness.*]

FANTASY CONVERSATION WITH THE WOMAN IN THE BLACK SEQUIN DRESS

GOT THE JOB

WOMAN 3 *is drinking at the table. She is slightly drunk and it is late. The* WAITER *is standing by the opposite wall watching her.*

WAITER: Excuse me, but are you alone?

WOMAN 3: Yes. Alone.

[*Pause.*]

Alone with my thoughts.

WAITER: Oh, with your thoughts.

WOMAN 3: The doors open and in they come. Do you see what I mean?

WAITER: I see a woman, waiting perhaps, with an empty seat right beside her. There's something about it, don't you think. Something quite different to your happy seat. Lucky seat. I'm jealous of your seat. [*Has a guess.*] Marline?

WOMAN 3: No. Janine.

WAITER: I was close.

49

WOMAN 3: But no I'm not Janine either. My real name is Madeline.

WAITER: Madeline and Jack.

WOMAN 3: Jack?

WAITER: Well not really. But Madeline and Jack. Jack the handy man.

WOMAN 3: Are you handy, are you?

WAITER: Well not really.

WOMAN 3: Madeline and Andrew.

WAITER: Andrew! You know I can't sleep at night because of women like you. And now here you are.

WOMAN 3: I am. On my way somewhere else as a matter of fact. I'm expecting a lift. And I can see that you are a good driver.

WAITER: Absolutely right. I'm good at that.

WOMAN 3: That's what I need.

WAITER: You'll be in good hands.

WOMAN 3: Let me see hold them out.

> [*He does. She peers across from her table. Neither move.*]

Large, clean, well trimmed, the hand of a man that everyone loves. The world loves you I cansee that.

WAITER: Now that I've got the job, how about refreshments.

WOMAN 3: I'll have a baby cham, I'm going to be thorough.

> [WOMAN 3 *saunters across.*]

WAITER: Fill up from the bottom of the tank.

WOMAN 3: I intend to fill up until the dial hits the top.

FANTASY DANCE 5: DRUNKEN WILD CELEBRATION

We hear music. The WAITER *swings* WOMAN 3 *around. They dance. All the others move into action. They dance across the stage and out the right exit. There is a feeling of drunken celebration.*

SEQUENCE E: RE-ENTERING THE WORLD

NIGHTMARE 7

WOMAN 4 *is asleep on the earth. She wakes.*

WOMAN 4: What's that! What was that scream?
  [*Pause.*]
  I thought I heard a scream.
  [*She looks behind her.*]
  I need a drink of water. I think I fell, or someone fell.
  [*Pause.*]
  I need some water.
  [*She takes a glass of water. She sits and drinks then leaves.*]

COUNTRY WALK 4: CITY JUNGLE

The following actions occur simultaneously. WOMAN 1 *and* WOMAN
3 *leave the stage through the two exit doors and walk out into the
auditorium. They each walk several curcuits of the auditorium.*
WOMAN 3 *speaks the text as* WOMAN 1 *does the actions (or as voice
over). At a front corner they stop for the line, "It's me in a dress",
spoken by* WOMAN 1. *The* WAITER *clears away the tables and
chairs.* WOMAN 2 *enters after the others have left. She dances, from
the left exit, across the stage and out the right exit. She carries the
owl and moves only from the waist down in her dance. The* MAN
*enters from the left exit door, goes to the centre front, examines the
floor and stands still, looking upstage.* WOMEN 3 *and* 1 *arrive back
on stage and disappear through the two exit doors.*

WOMAN 3: Undine's shoes hit the pavement her legs are in action.
  Undine can see out of her peripheral vision the buildings
  towering above her, she can see them gradually sliding past one

after another. They are all very similar she notes, but her eyes are fixed ahead (she is on her way to catch a train). Her legs are quite relaxed, in this particular dress her legs feel bare, she likes these shoes, shoes for walking she has heard herself say. I like shoes for walking, not just sensible but stylish shoes made as if just for her feet. The air of the jungle is questionable. She thinks yes a jungle, this is my jungle, out here danger lurks. I will continue to walk at the same determined pace no matter how deserted the street becomes. And the last lap of her journey she knows is deserted. But she will claim her space, not much to ask, three feet in every direction around her body, her parameters. The circumference, the perimeter. Leave that alone tigers. There's a city tree sliding past it's well cut back, more trunk than leaves. Maybe like me, she thinks, more trunk than leaves. She suddenly swings her arms wider, they cut across the rhythm of her ordered soldier's walk, they suddenly swing in a circle, she sighs. That went to four feet out. Her feet are working along the pavement, her forty year old feet. I've had my feet for such a long time, she thinks.

[*The two* WOMEN *stop and look across at each other. The* MAN *walks from the left exit to the centre front and stands with his back to the audience.*]

She looks sideways and sees a figure looking at her, she looks familiar she thinks. How old is she. What size is she. Who is she. Very quickly she thinks these thoughts until suddenly the answer releases over her lips ...

WOMAN 1: "It's me in a dress."

WOMAN 3: She looks at her watch, relaxes, she swings her arms again, flexes her shoulders, she thinks to herself like that big Japanese man Yjimbo in the Kurosawa movie, and she walks on.

THE REAL IS UNREAL

We hear music. The train appears from the right tunnel. WOMAN 4 *is aboard. It stops centre stage.* WOMAN 4 *rises and slowly gets off the train. She stops at the bottom of the stairs and looks at the spot where the* MAN *usually stands. The* MAN *turns front centre stage and goes and stands by the downstage left wall. We hear the following text (as voice over by* WOMAN 1). WOMAN 3 *enters in a slip and lies on the earth.*

WOMAN 1 [*voice over*]: The real is unreal
    the hidden is visable
    the inside is outside
    she is slipping outside
    she is slipping inside
    she is slipping on a gown
    she is slipping off a gown
    the picture
    can have in fact does have
    several meanings
    depending on what
    what the observer
    expects of it, brings to it.

THE WOMAN IN THE BLACK SEQUIN DRESS ENTERS THE NIGHTCLUB

ENTRANCE 9 – THE GRAPHIC DESCRIPTION

As WOMAN 4 *proceeds on her central path, the* WAITER *speaks the following text as she walks.*

WAITER: The woman who is now not so young, more middle aged, of an age which confuses the onlooker, dressed smartly in a svelte black sequin dress walks into the nightclub her eyes are held, she has not had a drink, she has not been to a nightclub for years. Almost immediately one is aware of the precariousness of her long journey from door to table. First there is the choice of which table, then there is the high sheen of the floor to traverse in her new dance shoes. But of course dance shoes were made to be partnered and at this stage there is no partner. She steps out feeling no doubt as if she is in an enormous desert through which she has to travel, without a drink. She appears to be breathing very shallowly, perhaps she is even holding her breath. Her face at present appears almost mask-like. She looks as if she could be a smoker or as if she has spent quite a deal of time inside. Her skin is very pale. Her eyes very dark even though they could be blue. She has identified the table and is travelling in that direction, which is to her left. At approximately half way from the door to the table something occurs which upsets her progress.

[*The* WOMAN *stops when she hears the* MAN'*s voice.*]

FANTASY CONVERSATION WITH THE WOMAN IN THE BLACK SEQUIN DRESS

THE GORGEOUS DRESS

WOMAN 4 *and the* MAN *speak the text. At first the* MAN *remains by the wall.* WOMAN 1 *appears at the window.*

MAN: If I may say so, your dress is gorgeous, like a night sky full of stars.

WOMAN 4: In fact what you see is what you get. I was longing to sit in a nightclub in an appropriate dress. I thought black with sequins would be absolutely right.

MAN: It fits perfectly as if it were made for you.

WOMAN 4: Well I believe it was.

MAN: Ah.

[*Pause. She raises her hand, which has a cigarette in it.*]

WOMAN 4: Would you light my cigarette?

[*The* MAN *walks over to her, feels for his lighter, discovers he hasn't one. The* WAITER *throws him his. Their hands touch as he lights the cigarette, then he steps back.*]

MAN: You can be deaf and blind, and if you touch something, you know it exists. Touch is so reliable.

[*Pause.*]

And are you happy now you are in a nightclub, wearing your dress?

WOMAN 4: Even as I talk to you my level of happiness which was low, rises as if from my toes it's coming up, not quickly, reluctantly, with a great deal of caution. It's about up to my ankles, at this moment.

MAN: I see my job as filling you from the ankles to the thighs. Do you think that is possible?

WOMAN 4: It may be.

MAN: Well I have to confess I am honoured and inspired and confident.

WOMAN 4: I feel confidence in your confidence.

UNDINE'S STORY PART TWO

We hear the following text (as voice over by WOMAN 3*).* WOMAN 2, *in the day dress, appears at the left exit with a glass of water and walks across and out the right exit.* WOMAN 4 *and the* MAN *walk upstage, get on the train and it leaves. We see* WOMAN 1 *at the window. The owl is perched on the window sill. Finally we see only* WOMAN 3, *who has entered and is now sitting on the earth.*

WOMAN 3 [*voice over*]: Undine thought reassuringly to herself, A follows C which follows B which follows A. Ah, ah yes that's it, that's true. Everything follows. Once upon a time there was a young girl etc. But there was a moment in the story – AND SHE WANDERED IN THE WILDERNESS FOR SEVEN YEARS. What happened to time here she wondered. It was as if the whole story was rotating around the wilderness, and her entering and leaving it. Where did that put the story with it's logical A.B.C.D. She sat and stared at the brick wall. And she saw that the brick wall was a part of a large forest which she was inside and outside was a street and then another brick wall.

[*We see* WOMAN 2 *at the window.*]

There were brick walls everywhere. She realised the suburbs were made of bricks. Which the wolf could not blow down. The inside was the outside, she remembered. The bricks the forest the walls the sky, entering and leaving. One minute seven years ...

[WOMAN 3 *lies back down. We see a film of the desert, at first the desert and then a pan up to include the horizon (1 min 30 sec).*]

THE END

".... we gain breadth of soul and wider horizons through vertical descent, through the inwardness of the image. It's puzzling peculiarity draws us down and in. The art of memory is an art of time, as work with memory always is. Unlike spiritual space travel that goes farther and farther 'out,' with freaking and peaking, highs and speed, the deepening of psychological space increases through slowness. The alchemists spoke of patience as a first quality of soul and considered soul-making the longest journey, *a via longissima*."

From *Falling Apart / Re-Visioning Psychology*
By James Hillman

The original production was developed in collaboration with the designer Jacqueline Everitt, the composer Elizabeth Drake, the cast Margaret Mills, Helen Herbertson, Natasha Herbert, Mary Sitarenos, Ian Scott, Greg Stone and the writer/director Jenny Kemp.

56